The Food St

JAMES C. OHLS AND
HAROLD BEEBOUT

THE
FOOD STAMP
PROGRAM
Design Tradeoffs, Policy, and Impacts

A Mathematica Policy
Research Study

THE URBAN INSTITUTE PRESS
Washington, D.C.

THE URBAN INSTITUTE PRESS
2100 M Street, N.W.
Washington, D.C. 20037

Library of Congress Cataloging in Publication Data

Ohls, James C.
    The food stamp program : design tradeoffs, policy, and impacts
James C. Ohls and Harold Beebout.
        p. cm.

    Includes bibliographical references.
    1. Food stamp program—United States.   2. Welfare recipients—United States.   I.
Beebout, Harold. II. Title.

HV696.F6035   1993   93-7222
363.8'82'0973—dc20   CIP

ISBN 0-87766-577-X (alk. paper)
ISBN 0-87766-576-1 (alk. paper; casebound)

Urban Institute books are printed on acid-free paper whenever possible.

Printed in the United States of America.

Distributed by
                University Press of America
4720 Boston Way   3 Henrietta Street
Lanham, MD 20706   London WC2E 8LU ENGLAND

The Urban Institute Press is a refereed press. Its Editorial Advisory Board makes publication decisions on the basis of referee reports solicited from recognized experts in the field. Established and supported by The Urban Institute, the Press disseminates policy research on important social and economic problems, not only by Institute staff but also by outside authors.

The Food Stamp Program: Design Tradeoffs, Policy, and Impacts, by James C. Ohls and Harold Beebout, is a Mathematica Policy Research study.

Conclusions are those of the authors and do not necessarily reflect the views of staff members, officers, trustees, advisory groups, or funders of The Urban Institute or Mathematica Policy Research.

ACKNOWLEDGMENTS

Early drafts of some chapters were written with funding from the U.S. Department of Agriculture, Food and Nutrition Service. The rest of the manuscript preparation, including all work on the policy recommendations chapters, was financed by Mathematica Policy Research. We thank both organizations for their support. All views expressed in the book are our own and do not necessarily reflect the positions of either of the supporting organizations.

We are greatly indebted to Christy Schmidt and Steven Carlson, who provided important suggestions on how to structure the book, as well as insightful comments on earlier drafts. Esther Miller, Judy Richter, and Liz Schaefer provided valuable data gathering and computational support. Useful comments were also made by Robert Dalrymple, Carole Trippe, Pat Doyle, and two unidentified reviewers of the manuscript for the Urban Institute Press. Thomas Good provided valuable editing support.

We also thank each of the individuals who agreed to be interviewed about the legislative process which sets food stamp policy. Valuable comments on an early draft of that material were received from Robert Fersh, Lynn Gallagher, Larry Goolsby, Robert Greenstein, Julia Isaacs, Bonny O'Neil, Julie Paradis, and Betty Jo Nelsen.

CONTENTS

Tables

Figures

FOREWORD

The Food Stamp Program can be regarded as the linchpin of the U.S. safety net. It is the only part of the public assistance system that has uniform federal standards and is open to all in need regardless of age, health, or family type. Public benefits and related issues have been at the heart of the Urban Institute's research and policy agenda since its birth 25 years ago. We are, therefore, proud to publish the first major book on the Food Stamp Program since Maurice MacDonald's landmark study published in 1977.

The authors' discussion of the Food Stamp Program is structured in terms of the policy tradeoffs that are inevitable in the design of any means-tested benefit programs: targeting versus disincentives to work, administrative accountability versus ease of access, nationwide standards versus state and local flexibility.

Public policy textbooks typically include only superficial treatments of these tradeoffs and the behavioral response issues they raise. Students in public policy schools will, therefore, find the Ohls-Beebout discussion extremely valuable as they seek to gain real insight into how benefit programs really work.

Policy and program analysts working on other benefit programs also will find this discussion useful in helping them recognize how these tradeoffs may be affecting the program for which they are responsible.

James Ohls and Harold Beebout are two of the best qualified and most experienced food stamp analysts in the country today, as well as close students of the political side of food stamp policymaking. They are, therefore, excellently suited to write a comprehensive assessment of the design and impacts of this important program.

This book will be a useful addition to the tools available to current and future policy and program analysts as they pursue the never-ending task of making our public benefit system more responsive to the needs of both beneficiaries and taxpayers.

William Gorham
President

Chapter One

THE CONTEXT

The Food Stamp Program is a central component of America's public assistance system. With annual outlays of $22 billion, it serves more than 25 million participants a month.[1] It offers the only form of assistance available nationwide to all households on the basis only of financial need, irrespective of family type, age, or disability.

For many low-income households, the Food Stamp Program represents a major share of their household resources. For a typical welfare family with children, food stamps provide 25 percent of the family's total purchasing power (U.S. Congress, House of Representatives, 1989). In states that offer relatively low Aid to Families with Dependent Children (AFDC) benefits, the proportion can be 50 percent or more (Congressional Research Service, 1987).

The basic structure of the current Food Stamp Program has been in place for nearly fifteen years; however, the program has evolved substantially during that time as policymakers have balanced competing program objectives against a background of political and economic changes nationwide. Most of the issues which have influenced the structure of the Food Stamp Program are common to other major assistance programs as well. The purpose of this book is to review program issues likely to be important to welfare program design in the coming years, using the Food Stamp Program as our example. The book is intended for both practitioners involved in policy development and students who wish to learn more about the design issues that shape U.S. welfare policy.

This is a book about benefit program design. Given that program budgets are always limited, and that programs embody incentives that can change the behavior of potential beneficiaries, design tradeoffs among conflicting program objectives are inevitable. To note just one example: the faster you make benefits decline as income rises, the higher the proportion of benefits you can put in the hands of the very poor, but the more you discourage beneficiaries from working for pay. How much should you compromise the goal of helping the neediest in order to address the goal of encouraging work? If these tradeoffs are not made by design they will be made by default, which can have major unintended and pernicious effects. Our tradeoff discussion is couched in terms of the Food Stamp Program, to provide concrete examples of the problems we raise and how they can be dealt with.

Before we proceed to our central theme, we outline the key programs that make up the U.S. income maintenance system, to place the Food Stamp Program within the wider income maintenance context.

THE U.S. LOW-INCOME ASSISTANCE SYSTEM

Assistance to low-income households in the United States is provided through numerous programs. Each program has its own objectives, its own eligibility criteria, its own benefit structure, and its own legislative oversight. Some are federal programs, some are federal-state programs, and some are strictly state and/or local. Table I.1 lists the six major public assistance programs targeted specifically toward poor people.[2]

The Food Stamp Program provides assistance to help low-income households obtain a nutritious diet. Benefits under the Food Stamp Program are entirely federally funded, but the costs of program administration are shared by the federal, state, and local levels of government. It is administered jointly by federal, state, and local governments. The Food Stamp Program served more than 22,000,000 people monthly in Fiscal Year 1991, the period covered by the table, and since then monthly participation has increased to more than 25,000,000.

Federal-level administrative responsibility for the Food Stamp Program is housed with the U.S. Department of Agriculture. Legislative oversight is provided by the House and Senate Agriculture Committees. The Food Stamp Program overlaps other assistance programs, providing benefits to many of the households who receive benefits under the other programs listed in Table I.1.

Aid to Families with Dependent Children (AFDC) is the program people usually have in mind when they refer to "welfare" in the United States. AFDC provides cash assistance to households with children. Most AFDC recipients are female single parents and their children; although two-parent households in which the principal wage earner is unemployed are also eligible for the program. The generosity of AFDC benefits varies according to eligibility levels set by each state. An average of 13 million persons per month were assisted by AFDC, at a combined federal and state cost of $23 billion in 1991.[3] At the federal level, the Administration for Children and Families of the U.S. Department of Health and Human Services has responsibility for the program. The lead congressional committees for AFDC are the House Committee on Ways and Means and the Senate Finance Committee.

General Assistance is the name given to the programs most states have, at the state and/or local level, to provide emergency cash assistance to individuals with no other means of support. The eligibility requirements of General Assistance are generally substantially tighter than those for food stamps and AFDC, and the numbers of people served are much lower. There is considerable overlap in clientele between the General Assistance Program and the Food Stamp Program. There is much less overlap between General Assistance and the other programs surveyed in this section. Since there is no federal involvement in the program, no federal agency or congressional committees are formally responsible for it.

Supplemental Security Income (SSI) is designed to provide assistance to low-income persons who because of age or disability cannot work. Basic levels of benefits are set and provided by the federal government. In some states, additional supplemental benefits are provided. In a typical month, this program serves about 5.2 million persons.[4] Federal oversight is provided by the Social Security Administration in the U.S. Department of Health and Human Services. The relevant congressional committees are the House Committee on Ways and Means and the Senate Finance Committee.

The Medicaid Program is designed to ensure access to adequate health care by low-income households who are aged, blind, or disabled, members of families with dependent children, and certain other pregnant women and children. The majority of the participants in the other programs discussed so far are eligible for Medicaid benefits as well.

Detailed Medicaid rules and benefit levels are determined at the state level and benefits are financed jointly by the state and federal governments. Medicaid serves 28 million persons per year at an annual cost of $94 billion, counting both federal and state payments.[5] Federal oversight is provided by the Health Care Financing Administration of the U.S. Department of Health and Human Services. The

Table I.1 MAJOR U.S. PUBLIC ASSISTANCE PROGRAMS TARGETED TO LOW-INCOME AMERICANS, FISCAL YEAR 1991

Program	Target Population	Monthly Number of Persons Served[a]	Annual Cost[b]	Federal Administrative Agency	Legislative Oversight Committees
Food Stamp Program	Low-income households needing food assistance.	22.6 million	$20.0 billion	USDA, Food and Nutrition Service	House and Senate Agriculture Committees
Aid to Families with Dependent Children (AFDC)	Dependent children deprived of parental support or care, and certain members of their households, needing financial assistance.	12.6 million	$22.9 billion	DHHS, Administration for Children and Families	House Committee on Ways and Means; Senate Finance Committee
General Assistance (GA)	Low-income individuals with no other means of support because of ineligibility for AFDC, SSI, and Emergency Assistance.	1.35 million[c]	$3.1 billion[d]	Not applicable.	Not applicable.
Supplemental Security Income (SSI)	Low-income individuals unable to work because of age or disability.	5.0 million[e]	$19.0 billion	DHHS, Social Security Administration	House Committee on Ways and Means; Senate Finance Committee
Medicaid	Households receiving SSI or AFDC and certain other low-income households.	28.3 million[f]	$94.3 billion	DHHS, Health Care Financing Administration	House Committee on Energy and Commerce; Senate Finance Committee

| Housing Assistance | Low income renter households who live in public housing or who receive direct or indirect rent subsidies for privately-owned units, and low income owner occupants who receive subsidized interest rates on their mortgages | 5.5 million | $16.9 billion | HUD | House Committee on Banking, Finance, and Urban Affairs; Senate Committee on Banking, Housing, and Urban Affairs |

Note: Table excludes programs that are not targeted specifically to the poor but provide substantial assistance to low-income households. These include the Social Security Program and the Unemployment Insurance Program.

a. Unless otherwise noted, this column contains the average number of persons served per month at the federal, state, and local levels in fiscal year 1991.

b. Unless otherwise noted, this column contains the actual amount spent on both benefits and administration at the federal, state, and local levels in fiscal year 1991.

c. This figure represents the reported number of recipients in only 37 states, since not all states both have a GA program and report the number of recipients.

d. This figure represents an estimate of benefit costs for calendar year 1991 plus reported annual administrative costs for some states and counties in various years (1988, 1989, or 1990).

e. This figure includes administrative costs of only federal and federally administered state supplementation programs. However, administrative costs of the state-administered programs are not expected to be significant, since state program benefits account for only 3 percent of total SSI benefits.

f. Since monthly data were not available, this figure represents one-twelfth of the unduplicated Medicaid caseload for all of fiscal year 1991. This somewhat overstates the monthly figures.

House Committee on Energy and Commerce and the Senate Finance Committee have federal jurisdiction over the program.

Housing assistance to the poor is provided mainly by the Section 8 New Construction and Substantial Rehabilitation Program and the Section 8 Existing Housing Program. The former provides subsidized rents for households renting rehabilitated or newly constructed low-income housing; the latter subsidizes rents for low-income households living in older privately owned housing. Other low income housing assistance programs include public housing and programs which subsidize interest costs for home owners. Together, the housing aid programs involve a cost of $16.9 billion per year financed by the federal government.[6] The programs are mainly operated by the U.S. Department of Housing and Urban Development and are under the jurisdiction of the House Committee on Banking, Finance, and Urban Affairs and the Senate Committee on Banking, Housing, and Urban Affairs.

In addition to the six major income-tester programs listed in Table I.1, there is the increasingly important earned income tax credit (EITC), which supplements the earnings of low-income heads of households and provided about $9 billion of benefits in 1991. There are also many other smaller programs targeted to the poor that help pay utility costs, provide subsidized school meals for children, and offer job skills training. Finally, three large public benefit programs, although not means tested, provide important financial support to low-income families: social security, Medicare, and unemployment insurance. Like the programs listed in Table I.1, these additional programs also have their own eligibility criteria, benefit formulae, and administrative structure.

No society starting afresh would design a public assistance system like the one that we currently have. The multiplicity of unintegrated programs leaves some needy households "lost in the cracks" and others with more total assistance than society intended. Multiple programs also lead to administrative duplication and lack of coordination. In light of these factors, one approach to developing policy recommendations with regard to any given public assistance program, such as food stamps, would be to develop a comprehensive "reform" package for all public assistance policy. The obvious advantage of this perspective is that it helps identify an overall "target" system to which society might ideally try to move.

An alternative perspective is to examine potential changes in individual programs, on the assumption that the rest of the public assistance system remains more or less the same. This second approach takes the point of view that wholesale change is unlikely and that it is more fruitful to examine program-specific reforms that are more likely to be implemented.

Most of the policy discussion and research activity related to the U.S. public assistance system during the past 20 years has focused on the second, or program-specific, approach, and it is this latter approach that we follow here. Most of this book focuses on individual aspects of income assistance policy as exemplified in the Food Stamp Program. It is this perspective that most of the relevant research and policy discussion has taken in the past, and it is this perspective that is likely to guide policy in the foreseeable future. The likelihood of wholesale change is exceedingly small, in our judgment, and it is far from clear that wholesale change is feasible or desirable. The technical issues involved in such wholesale change are too complex, the political constraints too formidable, and the implications too uncertain.

This does not mean that our discussion is irrelevant to any more global examination of the income maintenance system. The issues discussed in this book are just as central to developing a comprehensive, integrated public assistance policy as they are to improving the Food Stamp Program, or any benefit program, considered by itself. In Chapter VIII we draw upon insights obtained in earlier chapters to discuss the prospects for and desirability of more global change in the system.

THE BASIC OBJECTIVES OF PUBLIC ASSISTANCE AND TRADEOFFS AMONG THEM

In a private market-based economy such as in the United States, not everyone can provide for themselves adequately. Individuals may be unable to work (the elderly, the young, and the disabled), may not be able to find jobs, or may work at wage rates that are too low to meet the cost for basic consumption items such as food, clothing, and shelter. The challenge in developing a public assistance program within this context is to meet the needs of persons who cannot provide fully for themselves, while also limiting benefit costs to levels society is willing to pay and minimizing the perverse effects of public assistance on the incentive to get and keep a job for those who can be reasonably expected to work. Certain program objectives are widely accepted as important in achieving this overall goal:

- Targeting program benefits to households who need them the most.
- Ensuring that all households defined as needy by program rules have effective access to the program.
- Ensuring that benefit levels are adequate to meet the program's objectives.
- Administering the program accurately and equitably.
- Minimizing administrative costs.
- Maintaining incentives for those who can work to find and hold jobs and thus reduce welfare dependence.
- Allowing sufficient flexibility in program administration to take into account such local factors as the characteristics of recipients, population density, and economic conditions.
- Ensuring that program benefits are in a form that best serves the needs of recipients.

The problem is that these objectives conflict, making their application in specific contexts, and the priorities established among them, fraught with subjectivity. In addition, the likely or projected effects of alternative policies to achieve these goals are often unclear. Thus, there is often much room for debate about how these objectives can be best achieved. A key purpose of this book is to show how tradeoffs among these objectives have shaped the current Food Stamp Program and to identify the challenges they pose for its future.

The following discussion highlights the most important tradeoffs.

Benefit Targeting versus Program Access

Many different factors interact to determine a household's need. Income, assets, expenses for necessities, household size, age—all these are important, as are many other factors. The more factors are taken into account the more precisely benefits can be targeted to need, but the more complex the program becomes to administer.

Furthermore, requiring extensive information to determine need may defeat its own objective by making it more difficult for potential clients to apply and be accepted for the program. For instance, asking applicants to supply detailed information on their financial or other circumstances places relatively heavy reporting requirements on households, which many may be unable to meet. Similarly, obtaining and processing detailed information requires a relatively large amount of staff time, increasing administrative costs and reducing the funds available for benefits. Highly complex program eligibility rules also increase the likelihood of errors, reducing the accuracy with which a program is administered.

The choices made by the Food Stamp Program in these areas are discussed in detail in Chapters II and III.

Benefit Adequacy versus Available Resources

Poverty in America is pervasive and persistent. As of 1990, more than 13.5 percent of Americans were living below the poverty line, and two-thirds of poor families were below 75 percent of the poverty threshold.[7] These numbers highlight large unmet public assistance needs.

But helping the poor is but one among a multitude of public policy goals competing for limited resources, and intense pressures on Federal and state budgets in the 1980s often led to reduced welfare support levels. In AFDC, for instance, benefit levels in most states are well below the "need standards" that the states deem necessary for households to obtain basic consumption items.[8] And in the Food Stamp Program in the early 1980s, Congress reduced maximum benefits below the levels deemed necessary for households to obtain an adequate diet (as discussed in more detail in Chapter II). An important ongoing policy debate about food stamps and public assistance more generally has centered on balancing benefit adequacy with resource constraints.

Administrative Accuracy versus Access and Cost

Administrative accuracy requires accurate determination of eligibility and benefit amounts, and prevention of fraud. The more accurately the program is administered, other things equal, the better the targeting and the greater the taxpayer trust that tax dollars are going to households that legitimately need assistance.

It is important to ensure that clients supply assistance program staff with accurate information about their circumstances and that this information is processed correctly. It is also critical that program benefits not be misappropriated by program staff and others involved in transacting benefits. Depending on the nature of the benefits (discussed below), adherence to program regulations by businesses and financial institutions in transacting benefits is also important, as is elimination of "trafficking," where benefits are bought and sold illegally.

However, increasing the amount of information and documentation required of applicants reduces the number of households who can produce adequate documentation, increases the processing time between application and benefit receipt, and increases the staff resources needed to process the information—all of which reduce access and increase administrative costs. As discussed in Chapter IV, determining how best to balance accuracy, accessibility, and costs was a major focus of Food Stamp Program policy debates during the 1980s.

Access versus Administrative Cost

In order for a public assistance program to fully assist the target population, all eligible persons need effective access to program benefits. This objective requires that potential clients be made aware of the program and know how to apply, that offices be located conveniently and staffed appropriately, and that clients be able to comply with the procedural requirements of program participation.

Increasing advertising and other outreach activities, lengthening office hours, hiring a sufficient number of qualified staff to help clients, and performing home visits for clients who cannot come to a program office are all steps that can be taken to facilitate program participation. But all increase administrative costs and reduce funds available for program benefits.

Optimal Benefits Use versus Access and Benefit Adequacy

Many public programs for low-income households, including the Food Stamp Program, provide assistance with specific types of consumption needs, such as food, housing, and health care. As discussed in detail in Chapter II, various types of "in-kind" benefits—which link public assistance to specific types of consumption—reflect society's judgments that access to these types of goods by low-income households is particularly important, either to the households being assisted or to society as a whole.

However, if program participation is linked to purchasing a specified minimum level of a particular consumption item, it may discourage program participation by households that feel they do not need as much of that item as they are required to purchase, even though they are woefully short of income to meet other needs. Moreover, if the purchasing patterns required for participation do not match the specific needs of individual households, the in-kind nature of the benefit will reduce its value to the households, even if they use it all on the specified item.

Work Incentives versus Other Goals

An important objective of low-income assistance policy in the United States is to make sure that people who can work do work. But at least in the short run, this goal may conflict with ensuring access, targeting on those most in need, and minimizing costs. For instance, one way to maintain work incentives in a public assistance program is to allow recipients who begin to work to keep a significant portion of their earnings, rather than taxing most of those earnings away in the form of benefit reductions. However, lowering tax rates on earnings to foster work, holding total benefit outlays constant, reduces the generosity of benefits for those who have no earnings to supplement their benefits.

Programs that provide educational and training services to program clients are particularly subject to the potential conflict between employment incentives, access, and minimizing costs. Such services often require a substantial commitment of resources and do not always reduce net public-sector costs. In addition, mandating participation in employment and training as a condition for receiving assistance may reduce the participation of households unable or unwilling to meet this requirement, even if they are in extreme need.

State and Local Flexibility versus Other Goals

The efficiency of certain organizational and operational procedures may vary greatly according to office size and location. For instance, local food stamp offices range from small county welfare offices in sparsely populated rural areas to large inner-city welfare offices that serve caseloads of 10,000 or more households, and procedures appropriate for large offices may be overly bureaucratic in small ones. Similarly, the types of employment and training services appropriate in a strong local economy with a low unemployment rate may be quite different from those that can be effective in a stagnating economy. Local flexibility in operating national assistance programs may also facilitate efforts to coordinate federal programs effectively with assistance programs administered at the local level.

But allowing local flexibility reduces the ability of policy makers at the federal level to achieve national objectives. For instance, if local jurisdictions are allowed to set program procedures, the national goal of ensuring access may be compromised. And past experience has shown that decentralizing administrative decisions compromises the goal of maintaining equity across different areas of the country.

HOW THE FOOD STAMP PROGRAM WORKS

Households wanting assistance can apply to the Food Stamp Program at local offices throughout the country. Each county within a state contains a food stamp office; densely populated urban counties often contain multiple offices. Households that meet certain financial and other criteria (discussed in detail in subsequent chapters) are certified by the local offices to participate in the program and are issued monthly food stamp benefit coupons based on their household size and the net income they have available to purchase food.

Food stamp coupons can be used to purchase food items at any of 215,000 food outlets that participate in the program nationwide. These outlets redeem the coupons for money at local banks, which are then reimbursed through the Federal Reserve system.

At the federal level, the Food and Nutrition Service (FNS) of the U.S. Department of Agriculture develops and publishes the program regulations that implement the relevant congressional authorizing legislation. FNS also provides guidance and monitors overall program administration.

Day-to-day program operations are conducted by state and local governments. In some states, the Food Stamp Program is administered directly by local program office staffs who are state employees. In other states, the program is administered by local governments (typically counties) under state supervision. In most areas, the Food Stamp Program is administered jointly with the Aid to Families with Dependent Children (AFDC) and Medicaid programs, even though the two programs have different statutory and regulatory provisions at the federal level.

Program benefit outlays are paid for entirely by the federal government. The federal and state governments share the costs of administering the program, with the federal government reimbursing states at a matching rate of 50 percent for most administrative cost categories.

FOOD STAMP PROGRAM HISTORY[9]

The concept of distributing food stamps to low-income families dates back to the 1930s, when the government decided to dispose of surplus food stocks accumulated under legislation to stabilize farm prices in the wake of the Great Depression. The surplus, rather than being simply destroyed, was distributed to the poor.

This early benefit program had a two-color system of stamps. Persons who met the eligibility criteria for locally administered cash assistance programs could buy orange stamps, which could be used to buy any food items on a dollar-for-dollar basis. But orange stamps also entitled participants to free blue stamps. One dollar of blue stamps was issued for every two dollars of orange stamps purchased, with the additional purchasing power available through the blue stamps tied to specific commodities designated as surplus by the Secretary of Agriculture. Welfare agencies were instructed not to reduce the cash grants from other assistance programs to recipients of food stamps, in order to ensure that the increased purchasing power afforded by the blue stamps would not be lost through cash grant reductions.

The blue and orange plan never operated on a nationwide basis. At its peak in August 1942, it served about half the counties in the United States and 88 cities, areas that together contained close to two-thirds of the U.S. population (U.S. Congress, Senate, Committee on Agriculture, Nutrition, and Forestry, 1985). Requiring households to purchase a substantial proportion of food stamps with their own money placed heavy emphasis on encouraging food consumption, but it also significantly reduced access to the program, particularly among very poor households. Further, by making participation a local option and by basing eligibility for the food program on locally determined eligibility rules, this pre-World War II version of the Food Stamp Program placed heavy weight on local flexibility at the expense of nationwide access to the program. The initial program was terminated in 1943 as the demands of World War II reduced agricultural surpluses.

During the 1950s, Congress expressed much interest in reintroducing food stamps as a means of disposing of the persistent stockpiles of food accumulating under the government farm price support programs while assisting the needy in maintaining an adequate diet. However, the concept was resisted by the Eisenhower Administration as increasing welfare expenditures without increasing the quantity of food consumed by the needy, and no food stamp program was actually implemented during that period. Instead, an extensive commodities distribution program—the Needy Family Program—was established to distribute commodities to low-income households through local distribution centers. The distributed food included both commodities accumulated by the federal government under commodity price support programs and commodities purchased directly with funds appropriated for the Needy Family Program. At its post-World War II peak in 1971, the program was serving over four million households. However, it was widely criticized because of (1) the limited range of commodities; (2) fluctuating availability; and (3) logistical difficulties in storing and distributing the food.[10]

In 1961, the newly elected Kennedy Administration reintroduced food stamps in the form of a pilot program in which food stamps were substituted for the commodities program in eight test counties. The two-color stamp feature was not included. The Kennedy Administration opted for a single-stamp system, under which families determined to be eligible by state and local policies were able to buy food coupons up to a maximum, by paying a fraction of the face value of the coupons they purchased. The difference between the dollar value of the coupons and the amount of money the household had to pay for them was called the "bonus value" of the stamps. These bonus stamps functioned much like the earlier blue stamps, except that the bonus stamps were not restricted to surplus food. For the first time, an income-conditioned feature was built into the purchase requirement, whereby the price of the stamps rose as a participant's income rose. Benefits were based on two allotment schedules—one for Northern and Western states and another (lower) one for Southern states. The pilot program was eventually expanded to 31 areas.

With strong support from the Kennedy and Johnson Administrations and northern Democrats, the Food Stamp Act of 1964 (P.L. 88-525) made the pilot program an alternative to direct commodities distribution on a nationwide basis, although counties were still free not to operate either program. Northern Democrats achieved passage by supporting farm price supports in return for southern support for the Food Stamp Program. As before, eligibility was determined according to state welfare criteria. The purchase requirement, which was determined by the Department of Agriculture, varied by income and household size. The federal government paid all benefit costs, all federal administrative costs, and about 30 percent of state and local administrative costs.

Although the detailed operational procedures of the Kennedy program differed considerably from the earlier two-color stamp system, the purchase requirement feature of the new program retained the basic emphasis on stimulating food consumption as opposed to maximizing access. The previous emphasis on local flexibility was also retained.

In the years after the 1964 legislation, the existence of two parallel but alternative programs—the commodities distribution program and the Food Stamp Program—reflected a compromise between two competing goals: (1) disposing of commodities, and (2) providing nutritional assistance to low-income households. Although disposal of agricultural surpluses was still of primary importance, the 1964 Act placed the Food Stamp Program on a permanent legislative basis, from which food stamps have grown to their current prominence in the income support system.

After the 1964 Act, the Food Stamp Program operated without any major federal legislative changes through the end of the decade. This period saw a massive shift in the character of the nation's food assistance programs as more and more localities dropped direct commodities distribution in favor of the Food Stamp Program. In fiscal year 1965, the Food Stamp Program encompassed 110 project areas and covered 0.4 million participants. In fiscal year 1967, it grew to 838 project areas and 1.4 million persons, and in fiscal year 1969 it included 1,489 project areas and 2.9 million persons (U.S. Congress, 1985). Figure I.1 shows participation growth over this and subsequent periods.

The year 1968 saw a public outcry about hunger in America. A CBS Documentary, the "Poor People's Campaign," and a widely publicized report, "Hunger USA," focused public attention and recommended expanding access to the Food Stamp Program. By 1969, in response to this concern about domestic hunger, together with concern that state program regulations created differential access to the Food Stamp Program, the Nixon Administration proposed legislation that would have reduced local flexibility in order to increase program benefits and make them more uniform across the country. When the House Agriculture Committee blocked that legislation, the Nixon Administration implemented a number of administrative changes that had the effect of increasing benefits for most participating households. Subsequent legislation passed by the Congress in late 1970 strengthened the program further. Several key elements of that legislation are still in force: (1) uniform national income and asset eligibility standards; (2) a federal government obligation to pay 50 percent of the program's administrative cost; (3) the regular indexing of allot-

Figure I.1 FOOD STAMP PROGRAM PARTICIPATION, 1962–1992

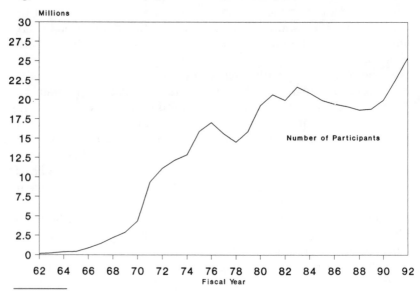

Source: See Appendix Table C.1
Note: Data do not include Puerto Rico.

ments and eligibility standards to take price changes into account; and (4) standard national maximum benefit schedules.

After 1970 the Food Stamp Program grew rapidly, as more localities chose to participate. From 4.3 million participants in 1970, the program grew to 9.4 million in 1971, to 11.1 million in 1972, to 12.2 million in 1973, and to 16.3 million in 1975.[11] The entry of Puerto Rico in 1975 completed geographic coverage.

By the second half of the 1970s, all states were required to serve all eligible people who applied for food stamps—making it essentially an entitlement program. Technically, the program was (and still is) subject to the annual appropriations process. However, Congress has always appropriated sufficient funds for full operation of the program, either through initial appropriations or through supplemental appropriations in years when the program was in danger of running out of money.

The next major food stamp legislation, the Food Stamp Act of 1977 (P.L. 95-113, Title XIII), eliminated the food stamp purchase requirement. During the 1970s, concern had been growing that participation was low because many needy households found it difficult to come up with the cash each month to pay the purchase requirement. Under the 1977 legislation, households received fewer coupons, but the dollar value of the subsidy remained the same, and households no longer had to pay anything out of their own pocket to obtain stamps.

Other provisions of the 1977 legislation illustrate the inevitable tradeoffs among different program objectives. A number of previously separate income deductions were consolidated, reducing the program's sensitivity to need differences among households in return for simplifying administration and reducing error. At the same time, however, the program sharpened its targeting by restricting the eligibility of college students and aliens, at the cost of counteracting the simplifying effect of the consolidation of deductions.

Elimination of the purchase requirement was the most recent change to the basic structure of the Food Stamp Program and added an estimated 3.6 million participants, with participation reaching an average of 19 million persons a month after it was implemented. During the 1980s, participation fluctuated around that figure, depending partly on economic conditions and partly on a continuing string of technical adjustments reflecting changing decisions on the tradeoffs discussed earlier in the chapter.

In 1979, legislation restored the medical deduction for elderly and disabled households, reflecting the judgment of Congress that elimination of this deduction in 1977 had gone too far in achieving program simplicity at the expense of targeting. It was viewed as politically unacceptable, in particular, to have elderly households declared ineligible for food stamps whose medical expenses were so high that they had less to spend on other necessities than many FSP participants.

The change in the political climate associated with the start of the Reagan Administration increased the policy emphasis on cost savings, accurate administration, and curtailing of fraud. Three legislative actions during 1981 and 1982 reduced program costs—including lowering program benefits directly, delaying inflation adjustments, reducing the earned income deduction, and reducing first-month benefits by prorating benefits from the day of the application. Moreover, additional income eligibility standards were added during this period to prevent relatively higher income households from qualifying through use of several different income deductions. Effectively, this change increased program complexity in order to reduce benefit costs by targeting eligibility more narrowly at the bottom of the income distribution.

Several changes in program administrative requirements were also made during the 1981–1982 period to reduce costs. They included (1) imposing financial penalties on states with high rates of errors leading to overpayment of benefits (high rates of underpayment were not penalized), and (2) requiring certain program participants to file monthly reports on their household income and household circumstances, thus fitting benefit amounts more closely to current need.

By the middle of the 1980s, the legislative emphasis shifted back toward increasing benefit levels and access. In 1984 and 1985, in particular, Congress passed legislation that restored previous cuts in maximum benefit levels and in the earned income deduction. Several other asset and income limits were liberalized at the same time. The 1985 legislation also enacted a major new food stamp employment and training program, aimed at getting able-bodied food stamp recipients into the work force.

In 1988, homelessness and hunger again moved into the limelight. In response, Congress passed the Hunger Prevention Act (P.L. 100-435) increasing benefit levels and making it easier for households to apply. It also placed greater emphasis on the effect of administrative errors resulting in underpayment of benefits (in addition to overpayments) in monitoring the administrative performance of the states.

OVERVIEW OF THE BOOK

As highlighted in this introductory chapter, developing public assistance policy requires continuing tradeoffs among various income maintenance program objectives. Chapters II–VI focus on key aspects of these choices and describe current food stamp policy in the areas affected by these tradeoffs.

Chapter II examines how recipient units and need are defined, and the form in which benefits are provided. The discussion focuses on targeting benefits to those who need them most versus keeping administrative costs and error rates low.

Chapter III examines food stamp participation rates and benefit levels. It also shows how program participation can be compromised by program features designed to meet other objectives.

A major focus of food stamp policy in the 1980s was to increase the accuracy of the eligibility and benefit determination process and to reduce program error rates—both politically sensitive issues. Chapter IV describes how these rates are monitored within the program and discusses a number of measures that have been taken to reduce them. The chapter also discusses cost-reduction initiatives that have been taken or proposed in recent years and how they can conflict with targeting objectives.

The Food Stamp Program's initial links to food expenditures and nutrition have become considerably weaker over time, due largely to efforts to increase access. Chapter V assesses the impacts of the current program structure on food expenditures and nutrition. A key issue in this regard is the extent to which changes designed to enhance access have weakened the program's ability to meet its food availability objectives.

Chapter VI discusses the impacts of the program on work incentives and employment. One important focus of this discussion is the trade-off between targeting program benefits to the most needy families and maintaining incentives for recipient households to work and reduce their dependence on assistance. The chapter also discusses the provision of employment and training services.

Through chapter VI, the book focuses on *what the possible choices are* among competing program objectives. Chapter VII provides a somewhat different perspective by examining *how choices are made* in setting Food Stamp Program policy. In particular, this chapter describes the political forces that shape Food Stamp Program policy and discusses the processes through which decisions are made.

Chapter VIII draws upon the analyses of the previous chapters to develop recommendations regarding future Food Stamp Program policy. These recommendations are discussed within the context of the trade-offs among policy objectives highlighted in earlier chapters.

Notes

1. Data for 1992 supplied by the U.S. Department of Agriculture, Food and Nutrition Service.

2. More comprehensive overviews of U.S. public assistance programs are provided by Mathematica Policy Research, Inc. (1990), and U.S. Congress, House of Representatives, Committee on Ways and Means (1992). The focus of this section is on assistance programs targeted to the poor. It is important to note, however, that several other assistance programs, while not specifically targeted to poor people, provide important support to low-income households. These include Social Security, Unemployment Insurance, and Medicare.

3. U.S. Congress, House of Representatives, Committee on Ways and Means, 1992, pp. 654, 657.

4. Calculated for fiscal year 1991 from U.S. Department of Health and Human Services, Social Security Administration, *Social Security Bulletin*, 1991–92.

5. Data on participants were supplied by the Health Care Financing Administration of the U.S. Department of Health and Human Services. Data on costs were obtained from U.S. Congress, House of Representatives, Committee on Ways and Means, 1992, p. 1652.

6. U.S. Congress, House of Representatives, Committee on Ways and Means, 1992, pp. 1679 and 1681.

7. U.S. Congress, House of Representatives, Committee on Ways and Means, 1992, p. 1,275 and U.S. Bureau of the Census, 1991, Table 20.

8. U.S. Congress, House of Representatives, Committee on Ways and Means, 1992, Tables 9 and 10, pp. 636–9.

9. This section provides a brief history of the Food Stamp Program to provide a context for the current policy issues discussed in later chapters. More detailed accounts are available in MacDonald (1977), U.S. Senate Committee on Agriculture, Nutrition, and Forestry (1985), and Berry (1984).

10. U.S. Department of Agriculture, Food and Nutrition Service (March 1983) contains a more in-depth discussion of the Needy Family Program.

11. U.S. Congress, Senate, Committee on Agriculture, Nutrition, and Forestry (1985).

Chapter Two

ISSUES AND TRADEOFFS IN DESIGNING ASSISTANCE PROGRAMS

In developing public assistance policy, society makes choices whether implicitly or explicitly, based on the tradeoffs highlighted in Chapter I. The degree to which these partially conflicting goals are met is determined by four crucial decisions about the structure of any assistance program:

- How the recipient unit is defined
- How the need for assistance is measured
- How benefit amounts are determined
- In what form program benefits are provided

Defining who is included in the recipient unit is a prerequisite to measuring need, since establishing financial criteria for program eligibility first requires identifying the persons whose needs are to be assessed. Measuring need is central to determining which potential recipient units are eligible for benefits. How assistance levels are determined defines how program benefits are targeted. Finally, the form of the benefits defines how much choice recipients have in using benefits. Cash can be used for any purpose; other forms of assistance are more restricted.

DEFINING THE RECIPIENT UNIT

The recipient unit can be defined as an individual person, related individuals who live together as a family, persons who share a common dwelling unit, or some other grouping. Different definitions have different implications for benefit targeting, administrative simplicity, and incentives for household formation.

If targeting benefits to those most in need is the main objective, the recipient unit is best defined as all persons who pool resources and make joint spending decisions. The alternative, defining the recipient unit as an individual, requires relatively arbitrary allocations of financial resources that are shared among household members, resulting in a somewhat arbitrary determination of neediness.

Defining the recipient household as the set of persons who make joint spending decisions also enables public assistance programs to take into account the reality that a group of individuals who live together can live more cheaply than the same set of persons living separately ("economies of scale"). In particular, it is possible to vary benefits per person by household size in order to achieve a better measure of need.

The basic concept of defining the recipient unit as the set of persons who make joint spending decisions is straightforward. However, implementing this concept in the context of the broad diversity of living arrangements that exist in the United States requires complex program rules to define household composition (discussed under "Applying the Household Definition").

In sharp contrast to targeting, administrative simplicity favors defining the recipient unit as an individual. This avoids the need for complex rules to determine who should and should not be counted in the recipient household—reducing both the time required by eligibility workers to identify the recipient household and the possibility of error.

How recipient units are defined can also affect living choices. Households may be tempted to exclude a potential member whose income or assets would make the rest of the household ineligible for assistance. Similarly, two groups who would otherwise share housing may choose to live as separate households if the program definition enables them to receive more benefits as two separate smaller households than as a single, larger household. The potential effects of recipient household definition on living choices are important, because incentives for households to split up artificially are destructive to family stability and increase total benefit payments inappropriately. Such incentives may be particularly counterproductive when there is a shortage of affordable housing.

The Recipient Household in the Food Stamp Program

The Food Stamp Program defines a recipient household as all members of a household who customarily purchase food and prepare their meals together. Persons who live alone and prepare their meals by

themselves are treated as one-person households. Program regulations presume that nonelderly close relatives who live together,
including spouses, parents, and siblings, share food. Thus, such relatives cannot apply separately for program benefits. It is important to
note that the Food Stamp Program definition of a household does
not necessarily include all the persons who live together in a single
dwelling unit. Persons who live at the same residence may not share
meals. If they do not and are not close relatives, they are not generally
considered to constitute the same food stamp household (with some
exceptions, as noted later).

This household definition is broader than those used by two other
important government assistance programs, AFDC and SSI. AFDC
limits the recipient unit to a set of children and their caregiving adult
or adults (usually the mother). Other residents of the dwelling unit,
such as the parents or siblings of an AFDC mother, are generally not
included in the AFDC unit, even though they may be considered
part of the recipient unit by the Food Stamp Program. The household
concept used by SSI is generally limited to the elderly or disabled
persons within a household and their spouses, even if they live with
other household members.

Applying the Household Definition

The detailed federal regulations that define households for the Food
Stamp Program, which require more than five pages of small print
to spell out fully,[1] reflect two basic sources of complexity:

■ Difficulties in applying the basic definition to the broad range of
possible living situations that exists in the United States
■ Attempts to exclude from the program persons or households not
targeted by the program within the intent of the law

APPLYING THE HOUSEHOLD DEFINITION TO VARIED
LIVING SITUATIONS

A typical household consists of a group of related individuals who
eat most of their meals together. For such a household, the Food
Stamp Program household definition is unambiguous. All the persons
in that household are considered a single recipient unit. However,
a number of household situations make this basic definition more
tenuous, including the following:

■ *Persons Who Eat Some but not Most of Their Meals Together*. In practice, there is a continuum of possibilities, ranging from household members who eat all their meals together to two or more people who share an apartment but eat all their meals separately. The program language opts out of deciding exactly where to draw the line with the phrase "customarily eat together."

■ *Boarders*. The food stamp application of a host household can include or exclude boarders, at the discretion of the host household. To define the types of situations for which this rule is applicable, the regulations contain detailed provisions about the financial arrangement that characterize true "arms length" boarders, as distinguished from persons who live together as part of the same household.

■ *Persons in Institutions*. In general, residents of institutions who receive most of their meals from the institution are not eligible for food stamp assistance. However, the law does extend food stamps to persons who reside in certain types of institutions that house groups which Congress has singled out as targets for stamp benefits: narcotics addicts or alcoholics in treatment centers, women and their children who live in shelters for battered women, residents of certain types of federally subsidized housing for the elderly, residents of nonprofit shelters for the homeless, and blind or otherwise disabled individuals who are residents of group living arrangements.

■ *The Homeless*. Food stamp regulations specifically allow persons without residential addresses to be certified for food stamps, using nonresidential addresses and authorized representatives through which they can be contacted.

■ *Elderly Persons Who Live with Close Relatives Due to Their Disabilities*. An elderly disabled parent who lives with his or her child can in some circumstances be counted as a separate food stamp household, *even* if the elderly parent and the child eat together. This rule seeks to avoid denying food stamps to elderly people who are forced to move in with their children because they can no longer care for themselves.

COMPLEXITIES INTRODUCED BY BENEFIT TARGETING CONSIDERATIONS

Certain groups of potential clients are singled out for special mention in the laws governing food stamp eligibility. Several instances of this phenomenon have already been noted as it pertains to special provisions for *including* certain groups in the program. But certain groups are specifically *excluded* from participating in the program. Most students enrolled in college or graduate school, for example, are explicitly excluded. However, this exclusion does not apply to students who work at least 20 hours a week or who are on AFDC. Persons who are on strike from a job and were not eligible for food stamps prior to the strike are also excluded from program participation, as are persons who have failed to comply with Food Stamp Program requirements to engage in education and training or employment programs.

ASSESSING NEED

A key policy objective in determining a household's need is to measure its ability to meet its consumption needs with its own financial resources. Two basic measures of financial resources are potentially important: *Income amounts* provide a measure of the flow of financial resources to a household over time; *asset levels* indicate whether a household has the financial resources to meet its needs, even if its current income is very low. Most assistance programs, including the Food Stamp Program, take into account both measures.

In measuring need, program designers must address the following issues:

- The measure of income, gross or net, that should be used
- The time period over which income is to be measured
- Income limits
- Asset limits

Gross versus Net Income

Gross income (or total income) provides a broad measure of the purchasing power available to a household. However, at least in the short run, many households do not have full spending discretion. In particular, necessities, including housing costs, utility payments, and medical expenses, may be largely beyond a household's control. The concept of *net income* seeks to take into account differences in the potential nondiscretionary expenses of households.

If the categories of expenditures subtracted from gross income to calculate net income reflect spending that is *fully beyond the household's control,* then net income is the better measure of true need. However, to the extent that the differences reflect the *consump-*

tion choices made by households on the basis of their individual tastes, then a gross income concept is the better measure.

The food stamp shelter deduction illustrates this point. Some differences in housing expenditures among low-income families reflect factors completely beyond their control, such as whether they have access to public housing. To the extent that this factor is at work, the net income concept, which "nets out" differences in housing costs, reflects differences in needs among families more accurately. However, variations in housing costs may also reflect the choices families make about the quality of their housing versus other consumption items. In this case, differences in expenditures reflect taste rather than need, and a gross income measure is more appropriate.

INCOME DEFINITIONS IN THE FOOD STAMP PROGRAM

In defining income for purposes of eligibility and benefit determination in the Food Stamp Program, Congress uses both the gross and the net income concepts. To be eligible for the program, most households (those without elderly or disabled members) must pass a gross income test, based on their overall income levels without deductions. However, households must also pass a net income test, which is based on an income measure computed by subtracting several deductions, including a shelter deduction, from gross income. As discussed in a later section, this net income concept also provides the basis for determining food stamp benefit *levels* for households who have been determined eligible.

The use of two different income tests resulted from dissatisfaction with the net income concept used during the 1970s. Households with relatively high incomes were (because of high deductions) passing the eligibility screen and receiving considerable media attention as exploiters of the system. Congress instituted the gross income test to prevent such cases from receiving food stamps. This also limited the future growth of the program and increased the program's participation rate, since participation rates tend to be lowest for households at the top of the income eligibility range (as discussed further in Chapter III).

TYPES OF INCOME INCLUDED IN GROSS INCOME

The objective of defining gross income for the Food Stamp Program is to include all revenue flows that accrue to a household and can be used to purchase food. With a few exceptions noted later, the program implements this principle by defining household gross income as the sum of the earned and unearned incomes of all members of the food stamp household.

Earnings include wages and salaries and self-employment income. Income from roomers and boarders and other rental income (if the property is self-managed) is treated as self-employment earnings. However, to help maintain incentives for household members to work, the Food Stamp Program definition of gross income excludes the earnings of students under 18, takes into account the work-related expenses of households with self-employment income, and excludes the cost of producing self-employment income. For farmers, self-employment losses (i.e., negative net income) can offset any positive income.

Unearned income is defined as cash receipts that are not earned, including payments from federal, state, and local assistance programs (such as AFDC, SSI, and veterans' benefits), as well as social security payments. Exceptions include (1) income considered as reimbursement for tuition and fees for postsecondary education and (2) energy assistance payments.

Allowable Deductions in Determining Net Income

Net income is computed by starting with gross income and subtracting out certain deductions allowed by the program rules. One key objective in defining the deductions is to restrict the definition of net income to reflect the resources that are truly available for purchasing food. Another is to preserve work incentives and to target benefits to particular recipient groups, especially the elderly and disabled. However, fully achieving these objectives conflicts with the goal of administrative simplicity.

The following formula is used to determine net income in the Food Stamp Program:

$$NY = (EARN + UNEARN) - STDDED - EARNDED - MEDDED - SHELDED - DEPDED,$$

where:

NY	=	Net income
$EARN$	=	Earnings
$UNEARN$	=	Unearned income
$STDDED$	=	A standard deduction available to all households

> EARNDED = An earned income deduction available to all house-
>   holds with earnings
> MEDDED   = A medical expense deduction, limited to the
>   elderly and disabled
> SHELDED = A shelter deduction available to households whose
>   shelter expenses are high relative to their income
> DEPDED   = A dependent-care deduction available to house-
>   holds who incur dependent-care costs associated
>   with work or training

The shelter deduction variable is itself defined in terms of the other variables in this equation. It is given by the formula:

> SHELDED = MINIMUM [CAP, EXPENSES − .5*(EARN
>   + UNEARN − STDDED − EARNDED − MEDDED −
>   DEPDED)]

where:

> EXPENSES = Shelter expenses, including rent, mortgage, and
>   utility payments
> CAP   = The maximum deduction[2]

The following discussion highlights key features of the allowable deductions in these formulas.

All households are allowed to take a *standard deduction*. As of January 1992, the amount of this deduction was $122. The standard deduction was enacted in 1977, as noted earlier, to simplify administration by replacing several other individually calculated deductions. It recognizes that most households have at least some nondiscretionary expenditures beyond those considered in the other deductions. Examples include tuition expenses, alimony and child support, and unusual expenses incurred due to disasters.[3]

The standard deduction, which is the same for all sizes of households, tends to have the greatest proportionate impact on smaller households. It also tends to have a relatively greater effect on households on the high side of the income range, since the lowest-income households often have zero net income, even in the absence of the standard deduction.

A second deduction applies to households with earnings, and is calculated as *20 percent of earned income*. One purpose of this deduction is to recognize the nondiscretionary work-related expenses of households, such as the costs of work clothes or commuting. In addition, in the context of the food stamp benefit-level determination process discussed later, this deduction helps maintain incentives for employment, because it reduces the effective tax rate on earnings in the program benefit formula.

An additional deduction for work-related expenses is the *dependent care deduction*. This deduction, which has a ceiling of $160 per dependent per month, is designed to reflect the costs of obtaining care for dependent children or disabled household members, to enable household members to hold jobs or engage in other employment or training activities. This deduction is also consistent both with making the net income concept reflect levels of discretionary income and with maintaining work incentives. Less than 2 percent of food stamp households claim a dependent care deduction.

The fourth deduction is the *medical expense deduction*. This deduction covers unreimbursed medical expenses that exceed $35 per month for elderly or disabled members of a household. That this deduction applies only to the elderly and disabled is consistent with more general concern for these groups in the Food Stamp Program rules. The $35 threshold factor greatly simplifies program administration by eliminating the calculation for households incurring only minor unreimbursed medical expenses during a month. About 3 percent of food stamp households claim a medical cost deduction.

Finally, households are allowed a *deduction for excess shelter costs*—including rent, mortgage payments, taxes, and utility expenses. "Excess" is defined as shelter costs that exceed one-half of gross income after each of the four previous deductions are subtracted. For most households, the maximum shelter deduction as of January 1992 was $194. Households that contain elderly or disabled members are exempt from this maximum.

In order to minimize administrative complexity, states have the option of applying a standard utility allowance in computing the utility component of shelter costs for households that incur heating or cooling expenses; thus, case workers need not obtain and apply information on each individual utility. To avoid penalizing households with extraordinary utility costs, actual utility costs can be used if they exceed the standardized amount.

The shelter deduction is by far the most commonly used deduction other than the standard deduction, and it is the most expensive to administer. In light of this, some observers have suggested eliminating it and increasing the standard deduction by the average size of the shelter deduction. This proposal has been resisted by northern and midwestern states on the grounds that the shelter deduction reflects differences in costs of living in different parts of the country.

The shelter deduction is most helpful to households in the middle of the eligible income range. Very poor households benefit relatively little from the shelter deduction, as with other deductions, because their net incomes, even without the shelter deduction, are very low. Higher-income participants benefit less from the shelter deduction, because the deduction is limited to shelter expenses that exceed half of income net of the other deductions and higher income recipients are less likely to be spending half their net income on housing.

Accounting Period

Another choice in establishing income-related eligibility criteria is the accounting period over which income is to be measured. Two key choices must be made: (1) the length of the period used to measure need and (2) whether estimates of need should be based on past income or on estimated future income.

LENGTH OF PERIOD

The shorter the accounting period, the more responsive the program is to changes in household circumstances. Suppose that someone in the food stamp household loses a job. From the standpoint of targeting assistance to households that need it, it is important that the lost household income be replaced at least partially with program benefits as soon as possible. But the frequent changes in program benefit levels stimulated by short accounting periods raise administrative complexity, administrative cost, and error rates.

PROSPECTIVE VERSUS RETROSPECTIVE ACCOUNTING

Under a prospective accounting approach, program eligibility and benefits for a given month are based on the expected income for that month. Under the retrospective approach, eligibility and benefits are based on actual income in some previous month, typically one or two months prior to the month for which the eligibility decision is made.

Ideally, the assistance received by a household in any given month should match its needs in that month. A prospective accounting period gets closer to this targeting objective because, in principle, prospective accounting makes it possible to provide assistance for any given month that corresponds directly to a household's expected needs in that month.

However, prospective accounting is less attractive administratively, because it requires judgments about whether past sources of income are likely to continue in the future. Mistaken expectations lead to over- or underpayments. Under retrospective accounting, the actual amount of income received in a previous month is known. Thus, using data from a previous period leads to fewer errors and less need for adjustment. Using retrospective data is also less expensive administratively because case workers need not devote time to making judgments about expected income flows.

THE ACCOUNTING PERIOD IN THE FOOD STAMP PROGRAM

The Food Stamp Program allows states to choose the accounting period for an ongoing food stamp case. A prospective accounting period is used for all new applicants, however, to ensure that households applying to the program with no current financial resources are able to receive immediate assistance.

The accounting period distinction is further complicated in the Food Stamp Program because states have the option of determining *benefits* on a retrospective basis but determining *eligibility* on a prospective basis. The objective of the latter is that food stamp assistance can be stopped immediately, when a household's income puts it over the cutoff point.

The accounting period issue provides a good example of the complex interactions among different program objectives. A prospective accounting period provides the flexibility to target benefits to those who need them the most, but administrative considerations have prompted the program to rely more heavily on a retrospective approach. Some of the obvious targeting problems caused by the retrospective approach have been corrected with several additional program provisions (prospective budgeting for new cases and the option of prospective accounting for eligibility). But these partially counteract the error reductions and administrative cost savings of retrospective accounting. The data are not available to estimate the net effect of these tradeoffs.

Establishing Income Limits for Program Eligibility

Income limits for establishing program eligibility are another important program parameter. On the one hand, other things equal, the program should be made available to all who need it; on the other hand, in a world of limited resources, eligibility must be defined narrowly enough to direct those resources to the households who need them the most. There is no obviously "correct" definition of who "needs" assistance. Rather, a continuum of need exists. Choosing the point on that continuum at which the eligibility cutoff line should be drawn is unavoidably a value judgment, as expressed through the political process.

Further ambiguity is introduced by the relationship between measured income and "true need." Due to different tastes and life styles, as well as other factors, one family with a given income and asset level may consider itself—and may be perceived by others—to have an acceptable level of financial resources, while a second family with the same income and assets may consider itself—and be perceived by others—to need assistance. The income deductions incorporated into the program's net income definitions take differences in household needs into account to some degree. But they are a blunt instrument that misses subtle differences in the needs of different households.

In the context of these ambiguities, one possible approach for setting assistance program income cutoff limits is to base them on the federal income poverty levels used by the Bureau of the Census for statistical reporting purposes. These standards were first developed in 1964 and were originally based on estimates of the food expenditures required by low-income households to obtain adequate food. Three times the required food expenditures, which varied by household size and composition, was designated as the poverty standard, based on data showing that families spent, on average, about one-third of their income on food. The poverty index is stated in terms of annual income levels and is updated every year, based on changes in the Consumer Price Index.

Using the federal poverty levels for setting income cutoff levels for an assistance program is attractive, since these levels represent an external, widely accepted measure of which households in American society are poor and thus need assistance. However, using the poverty thresholds does not fully avoid the conceptual ambiguities discussed earlier, since the poverty levels themselves are based on numerous assumptions and judgmental factors, which may not correspond to targeting objectives of a specific program. As will be discussed later, the Food Stamp Program income cutoffs are based only in part on the poverty thresholds.

FOOD STAMP INCOME CUTOFF LEVELS FOR ELIGIBILITY

The Food Stamp Program's net income eligibility cutoff level is 100 percent of the federal income poverty level for any given household

Table II.1 SUMMARY OF INCOME-RELATED ELIGIBILITY RULES, AS OF
           JANUARY, 1992

Accounting Period	
New Cases	One-month; prospective accounting
Old Cases	One-month; either prospective or retrospective at state option
Types of Income Included	
Earned Income	Wages and salaries; income from farm or business
Unearned Income	AFDC benefits, Social Security benefits, General Assistance benefits, and income from assets
Allowable Deductions in Computing Net Income	
Standard Deduction	$122 per household
Earned Income Deduction	20 percent of earned income
Excess Shelter Costs	Shelter costs in excess of half of net income; capped at $194[a]
Medical Deduction	Unreimbursed medical expenses in excess of $35[b]
Dependent Care Expenses	Cost of caring for a dependent to allow food stamp participants to hold jobs or to go to job training programs; capped at $160 per dependent
Income Limits	
Net Income	100 percent of poverty line
Gross Income	130 percent of poverty line

a. Cap is not applicable to households with elderly or disabled members.
b. Applicable only to households with elderly or disabled members.

size. Since the poverty level is a gross income concept, this puts the
food stamp income cutoff level *above* the official poverty line. The
gross income cutoff criterion of 130 percent of the poverty level is
applied to households that do not contain an elderly or disabled
member.[4] Both these cutoffs reflect a political judgment that the
official poverty levels do not adequately define need from the Food
Stamp Program's viewpoint. In addition, as noted above, the poverty
standards are defined in terms of annual income, while the Food
Stamp Program regulations focus on monthly income. This discrepancy is another wedge between the income concepts developed for
statistical measurement and those developed to accomplish the specific goals of the Food Stamp Program.

Table II.1 summarizes the income-related rules for eligibility determination.

Assets-Related Criteria for Program Eligibility

The key objective in establishing assets-related criteria for program eligibility is to identify the spendable resources represented by a households' assets.

ASSETS FOR DEFINING ELIGIBILITY

There is little question that liquid financial assets, such as bank accounts, stocks, and bonds, should be counted toward program eligibility. These financial instruments are readily convertible into direct purchasing power, and their use does not interfere directly with other aspects of a household's life.

Less obvious is how real estate should be treated. On the one hand, selling real estate to meet short-term needs may be difficult due to constraints on selling property quickly. In addition, given that home ownership is widely perceived as important for long-term family stability, forcing households to sell their homes in order to deal with periods of temporary need may be contrary to the public interest. Moreover, imposing such a condition could discourage the participation of many households whom most people would consider in genuine need of assistance.

On the other hand, the objective of targeting program benefits to those most in need of them would argue *for* counting a household's home equity toward program eligibility. In particular, a household who has built up a substantial amount of home equity has more financial options than does a renter household with comparable income. Because budget constraints limit the degree to which all needs of all households can be met fully (as discussed in detail in the next chapter), a legitimate question is whether an assistance program should stop short of meeting all the legitimate needs of very needy households in order to assist households with considerable home equity resources to draw upon.

Similar considerations apply to vehicles. On the one hand, a household with a car clearly has more resources than a similarly situated household without a car. On the other hand, given the distances from place to place and the lack of public transportation in many suburban and rural settings, having to sell the car to qualify for assistance could prevent household members from getting or keeping a job.

ESTABLISHING ASSETS LIMITS

From the standpoint of administrative efficiency, asset limits should be sufficiently high that most potential client households are not frequently crossing back and forth across the eligibility threshold because of normal within-month variations in cash flow. Encouraging financial independence also argues for allowing households to acquire at least some assets without losing program eligibility, to enable them to save for security deposits on apartments, or other needs that require significant expenditures. Counterbalancing these factors, as always, is the objective of targeting program resources to households most in need.

THE FOOD STAMP PROGRAM ASSETS TEST

The Food Stamp Program includes all financial assets. It excludes homes; one car unless its fair market value exceeds $4,500; and vehicles used to produce income, to transport handicapped individuals, or to travel long distances for work-related reasons.

The Food Stamp Program household asset limit for eligibility is $2,000 for households without an elderly member and $3,000 for households with an elderly member. These limits apply to all households regardless of size.

One implication of the Food Stamp Program's asset limits is that, in effect, a household must "spend down" most of its savings to become eligible for food stamp assistance. While the spend-down of savings is consistent with targeting food stamps to those who have the most immediate need for assistance, it has been criticized as limiting the program's effectiveness at serving the temporary needs of persons who lose their jobs during periods of high unemployment. It has also been criticized as unfair to households who have accumulated savings but now have them threatened by temporary income loss. The somewhat higher asset cutoff limit for households that contain elderly members may partially reflect this concern.

DETERMINING PROGRAM BENEFIT LEVELS

Two key principles are applied in most low-income assistance programs, including the Food Stamp Program: (1) that benefits be related to need as reflected by income levels, with the poorest households receiving the greatest amount of assistance (vertical equity), and (2) that households with a similar amount of financial resources receive the same level of assistance (horizontal equity).

Within this context, determining program benefits involves three key issues:

■ Setting the maximum benefit levels for households with no income;

■ Setting the rate at which benefits will be reduced as income increases (this is conceptually the same as the tax rate on earnings and other income); and

■ Adjusting benefit levels for changes in the overall price level over time.

Criteria for Setting Maximum Benefit Levels

Central to setting benefit levels are tradeoffs between benefit adequacy and costs. The higher the benefits the more people can be helped but the more the program will cost.

Targeting and administrative issues are also important in setting maximum benefit levels. Need varies by household size and the characteristics of household members, such as their age and gender, but taking account of these factors complicates program administration. In particular, increasing the number of variables used to determine benefit levels increases both program costs and error rates, by increasing the amount of information that must be obtained and applied in the benefit determination process. Increased information requirements also reduce program access by making it more difficult for potential program participants to provide the necessary documentation.

THE DETERMINATION OF BENEFITS IN THE FOOD STAMP PROGRAM: OVERVIEW

Program benefits for Food Stamp Program participants are calculated according to the following formula:

$$B = MAX - .3(NY)$$

where:

B	=	food stamp benefits[5]
MAX	=	the maximum benefit amount
NY	=	net income, as calculated according to the formula presented in Section 1
.3	=	the rate at which benefits are reduced with increased income

Reflecting the program's goal of providing food assistance, the Food Stamp Program's maximum benefit levels are designed to allow participant households to purchase a low-cost nutritious diet. In particular, the maximum program benefit levels are based on the estimated costs of purchasing a relatively inexpensive set of foods that allow household members to meet the Recommended Daily Allowances (RDA) for key nutrients—as published by the U.S. National Academy of Sciences (National Academy of Sciences, 1980)—without departing drastically from the typical food buying habits of low-income Americans.

In order to operationalize this goal, the Food Stamp Program relies on findings from research conducted by the Human Nutrition Information Service (HNIS) of the U.S. Department of Agriculture. HNIS has developed four food purchasing plans, each of which is based on the RDA levels and on typical food-purchasing patterns for four income groups—as observed in a 1977–78 survey of food use in the United States. Each plan specifies the amounts of a particular list of foods that households require to provide nutritious diets for their members. The four food lists provide the same nutrition, but at different costs. The maximum benefit levels for the Food Stamp Program are based on the least expensive of the four plans, the Thrifty Food Plan.[6] The food composition of the Thrifty Food Plan was last updated in 1983.

Prior to 1982, maximum benefits were set at 100 percent of the Thrifty Food Plan levels. In 1982, in the general political climate of retrenchment, cost-of-living adjustments were delayed and the maximum levels lowered to 99 percent of the Thrifty Food Plan amounts. Legislation passed in 1984 restored the earlier maximum, and legislation in 1988 established a schedule for increasing the maximum benefit levels to their current amounts, which are 103 percent of the Thrifty Food Plan.

Use of the Thrifty Food Plan to set food stamp benefits involves judgments, both in developing the Thrifty Food Plan itself and in developing the RDAs on which it is based. With respect to the RDAs, available scientific evidence on human nutritional requirements does not provide conclusive evidence for determining minimum requirements. Thus, the RDA requirements must be viewed as reflecting the *best judgments* of scientific panels rather than as established scientific facts. Indeed, the appropriate allowances to be set for certain nutrients are quite controversial (Community Nutrition Institute, March 8, 1990).

With respect to the Thrifty Food Plan itself, it would be possible to meet the RDAs with very low food expenditures. However, since the foods included in such a diet would not be considered palatable by most Americans, the actual foods included in the Thrifty Food Plan have been chosen, at a somewhat higher cost, to approximate the food consumption patterns of low-income Americans.

The issue of how to set maximum program benefits illustrates a tension between viewing the Food Stamp Program as an income maintenance program and viewing it as a food assistance program. The benefit structure based on the Thrifty Food Plan has considerable logic when the program is viewed as a nutrition program. However, this method of benefit determination is essentially arbitrary if the program is viewed as an income assistance program.

So far, most active participants in the food stamp policy setting process have chosen to focus the issue within the context of the Thrifty Food Plan. Conservatives have done so largely because they view the program as a nutrition program, and liberals have taken this approach, at least in part, because associating the program as closely as possible with food provides political protection against benefit cuts. (See Chapter VII.) However, the limited success of the Food Stamp Program, when considered in conjunction with other assistance programs, in raising American households out of poverty raises broader issues about benefit adequacy (discussed further in Chapter IV).

ADJUSTING FOR HOUSEHOLD SIZE

The maximum program benefit levels in the Food Stamp Program are adjusted for household size. The Food and Nutrition Service bases these adjustments on survey data on the food expenditures of households of various sizes. As shown in Table II.2, maximum benefit levels increase with household size. However, the rate of increase is generally less than proportional, so that maximum benefits per person tend to fall as household size increases. This reduction reflects evidence that larger households can purchase and prepare food more efficiently than can smaller ones.[7]

For Food Stamp Program benefits to be based strictly on the Thrifty Food Plan, benefits should also be adjusted for age and gender of household members. Because of differing nutritional needs, for example, the average weekly cost of the Thrifty Food Plan for the typical household with a mother and two small children was $51 in December 1990, compared to $68 for two parents and a teenage son (see Table II.3).

Table II.2 HOUSEHOLD MAXIMUM BENEFITS AND PER PERSON MAXIMUM BENEFITS BY HOUSEHOLD SIZE: JANUARY, 1992

	Household Size						
	1	2	3	4	5	6	7
Household Maximum Benefit	$111.00	$203.00	$292.00	$370.00	$440.00	$528.00	$584.00
Per Person Maximum Benefit	$111.00	$101.50	$97.33	$92.50	$88.00	$88.00	$83.42
Per Person Maximum Benefit as Percent of One-Person House-hold Amount	100%	91%	88%	83%	79%	79%	75%

Source: U.S. Congress, House of Representatives, Committee on Ways and Means, 1992, p. 1624.

Table II.3 ESTIMATED COSTS OF THRIFTY FOOD PLAN, BY HOUSEHOLD SIZE
AND COMPOSITION, DECEMBER 1990

Household Composition	Approximate Weekly Costs of the Thrifty Food Plan
One-Person Household	
Male Age 60	$25.08
Female Age 60	$24.72
Two-Person Households	
Female and Male, Both Age 30	$48.10
Three-Person Households	
Female Age 30, Two Children Age 3–5	$50.61
Female Age 30, Male Age 30, Male Age 17	$68.35
Four-Person Household	
Male Age 40, Female Age 40, Two Children, Age 10 and 11	$80.10

Source: U.S. Department of Agriculture, Human Nutrition Information Service, 1990.

These adjustments are not made in food stamp benefits, however, because a considerably more complex benefit formula would be needed. In automated food stamp offices the computational change would not add much to administrative costs. But in offices where the calculations are still done manually, the extra cost would be considerable. And irrespective of the degree of automation, the need to obtain and record detailed age and gender information would substantially increase error. The decision not to adjust for age and gender has been supported by the courts (Rodway versus U.S. Department of Agriculture, 1975).

Changing the food stamp benefit formula to reflect such adjustments would also be extremely unpopular politically, because age/gender adjustments would reduce the benefits going to babies, young children, and the elderly relative to the benefits going to prime-age men and teenagers.

Setting Benefit Reduction Rates

The rate at which benefits in income-tested programs are reduced as earnings increase is referred to as the "benefit reduction rate." If program benefits are reduced by 75 cents as a result of another dollar of earnings, for example, the benefit reduction rate is 75 percent.

This rate is effectively a tax on earnings. If a household on assistance makes an additional dollar of earnings, but then experiences a 75 cent reduction in assistance payments, its net increase in purchasing power from the dollar increase in earnings is only 25 cents. Thus, 75 percent of the increase in earnings is "taxed" away by the program. The terms "benefit reduction rate" and "program tax rate" are used interchangeably in our discussion.

Determining the appropriate benefit reduction rate for the benefit computation structure involves three major considerations:

- Targeting benefits to households that need them the most
- Controlling program costs
- Preserving work incentives

Targeting to greatest need and cost control both argue for reducing benefits rapidly as income rises. Preserving work incentives, however, argues for low benefit reduction rates. The higher the penalty for working, the lower the incentive to find or hold a job. At the limit, if benefits are reduced dollar for dollar with increases in earnings, a household has no financial incentive to work unless its earnings would be high enough to allow it to leave the assistance program entirely.

Figure II.1 illustrates the point about work incentives. The first panel of the diagram illustrates a household in an assistance program that imposes a 100 percent tax rate on earnings. The dashed line of the diagram shows earnings for different hours of work. The solid line shows benefit receipts. The dotted line shows net income. A household that works zero hours receives benefits equal to G. If benefits are reduced dollar for dollar with earnings, then total income, counting both benefits and earnings, does not increase until benefits drop to zero. The household has no financial incentive to work in the range between zero hours and the hours denoted by B1 in the diagram.

The second panel of the diagram illustrates the same guarantee level but a lower benefit reduction rate. Total net receipts increase with additional work effort throughout the range of possible hours of work. The point at which program benefits drop to zero is not reached until a higher hours level than in Panel 1, however, denoted by B2. Benefit targeting may be less precise, since households with relatively lower levels of need receive benefits; total program costs are higher; but work incentives are preserved.

Another issue associated with benefit reduction rates and work incentives pertains to the interaction among the maximum benefit level, the benefit reduction rate, and the income cutoff level for

Figure II.1 EARNINGS AND NET RECEIPTS BY HOURS WORKED

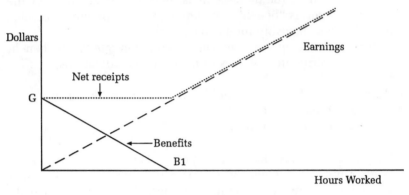

PANEL 1: 100% BENEFIT REDUCTION RATE

PANEL 2: 50% BENEFIT REDUCTION RATE

establishing program eligibility. Unless program benefits are at very low levels at the income *eligibility* cutoff, a "notch" effect occurs, with tax rates greater than 100 percent and extreme work disincentives.

Figure II.2 illustrates this potential problem. The figure is based on the same benefit reduction rate assumption as in the second panel of Figure II.1. However, in this new figure, the income cutoff limit for program eligibility, L, is reached at a level of earnings lower than that implied by the hours of work at which the benefit reduction rate has reduced benefits to zero. As shown, when this income eligibility limit is reached at B3 hours worked, net receipts by the household are reduced sharply—that is, notched—because benefits abruptly stop.[8]

Figure II.2 POTENTIAL "NOTCH" EFFECT

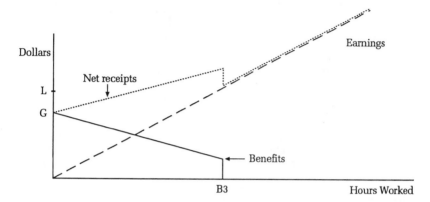

BENEFIT REDUCTION RATES IN THE FOOD STAMP PROGRAM

The current Food Stamp Program specifies a 30 percent benefit reduction rate. That is, a household's benefits are calculated as the maximum benefit level for the household (i.e., 103 percent of the Thrifty Food Plan adjusted for household size) minus 30 percent of the household's net income. But the *effective* benefit reduction rate is not always 30 percent because, as already noted, two of the deductions used to compute net income are themselves related to income— an earned income deduction from gross income of 20 percent, and a shelter deduction calculated as the excess of shelter costs above 50 percent of net income after other deductions are taken.

These features imply effective program tax rates on household earnings of 24 percent for households who do not have a shelter deduction and 36 percent for households who do.[9] Table II.4 shows the effects of a $100 increase in wages for two households—one ineligible and the other eligible for the shelter deduction. For the first household, wage income has risen by $100. The earned income deduction, allows $20 to be subtracted from net income, so the increase in net income is $80. Applying the 30 percent benefit reduction rate to this change reduces food stamp benefits by $24—implying that 24 percent of the initial wage increase is "taxed away."

The analogous calculations for a household with the shelter deduction are more complicated. As with the first household, the $100 increase in wages increases the earned income deduction to $20 yielding a net income increase of $80. However, the shelter deduction

Table II.4 CALCULATION OF IMPLICIT TAX RATES ON INCOME FOR FOOD
STAMP BENEFITS

		Household 1 (No Shelter Deduction)	Household 2 (Shelter Deduction)
1.	Increase in earned income	+ $100	+ $100
2.	Change in earned income deduction	+ $20	+ $20
3.	Increase in net income as used in the calculation of the shelter deduction	NA	+ $80
4.	Change in shelter deduction	NA	− $40
5.	Net change in deductions	+ $20	− $20
6.	Increase in net income	+ $80	+ $120
7.	Change in benefits	− $24	− $36

Line 2 = Calculated as 20 percent of earned income.
Line 3 = Calculated as Line 1 − Line 2.
Line 4 = For a household eligible for the shelter deduction, the shelter deduction is
computed as $H - .5 (Y - D_i)$, where H is housing costs, Y is gross income, and D_i
are other deductions. As Y goes up, the shelter deduction declines by .5 times the
change in net income, prior to the shelter deduction.
Line 5 = Calculated as Line 2 + Line 4.
Line 6 = Calculated as Line 1 − Line 5.
Line 7 = Calculated as .3 * Line 6.
NA = Not applicable.

is computed as the excess in shelter costs above 50 percent of the
household's net income prior to the shelter deduction. This means
that the shelter deduction is reduced by 50 percent of the amount
of the household's change in net income *after* the earned income
deduction. Thus, the change in the shelter deduction is .5 times $80,
or $40, and the household's overall increase in net income is $100
(wages) minus $20 (earned income deduction) plus $40 (shelter
deduction). These factors yield an overall increase in net income of
$120. Applying the 30 percent benefit reduction rate to this amount
reduces food stamp benefits by $36—36 percent of the wage increase
is "taxed away."

Since, by definition, there is no earned income deduction on
unearned income, the effective tax rates on unearned income are
higher. They are the statutory 30 percent for households without a
shelter deduction and 45 percent for households that have a shelter
deduction.

This discussion of effective tax rates has focused only on Food
Stamp Program rules. As will be discussed in detail later, many Food
Stamp Program participants receive assistance from other programs

that also reduce benefits (i.e., impose a tax) as household income rises. The combined benefit reduction rate faced by multiple-benefit households depends on how the program benefit formulae interact.

To be sure, the net income calculations for the Food Stamp Program include income from other benefit programs, so the combined tax rate is not as high as the sum of the separate rates. Nevertheless, the combined tax rate for a household participating in multiple programs can be very high.[10]

This overall discussion illustrates an added layer of complexity in developing programs to assist low-income households. Taken by itself, the explicit tax rate in the Food Stamp Program is 30 percent, and this is the tax rate that is usually considered in discussions about food stamp policy. However, the interactions among variables in the Food Stamp Program benefit formula yields a different effective tax rate for many program participants. And the effective tax rate on low- income households who participate in multiple programs can be substantially greater than 30 percent and, indeed, can sometimes approach 100 percent.

NOTCH EFFECTS

As noted earlier, the income cutoffs for food stamp eligibility are based on federal income poverty levels, which are not directly related to the Thrifty Food Plan on which benefits are based. Thus, the benefit reduction rate is the only tool available to keep benefit levels and eligibility cutoffs in line with each other in a way that avoids serious notch problems. The current benefit reduction rate serves this purpose moderately well. No notch exists for small households in the Food Stamp Program. Indeed, for one- and two-person households, the eligibility limit is *higher* than the income at which benefits calculated according to the standard formula would go to zero. In practice, no eligible household receives zero benefits because a program statute sets $10 per month as the minimum benefit for eligible one- and two-person households.

Notch effects do appear in the Food Stamp Program as household size increases, because larger households reach the net income eligibility cutoff before their incomes reach the zero benefit level. For a 6-person household in early 1991, for instance, the net income eligibility limit was $1,415 per month. At that level of income, monthly benefits were $77. Thus, a member of such a household could cause the family to lose $77 food stamp benefits by earning one extra dollar.

Adjustments for Inflation

As prices rise over time, the purchasing power conveyed by a fixed-dollar benefit level declines. Consequently, if real benefit levels are to be maintained, inflation adjustments are required. A very important issue in the design of any public assistance program is whether these adjustments should be made through periodic legislation or whether they should be built directly into the program through automatic cost-of-living adjustments. The latter ensure that real benefits do not decline, but they remove the opportunity for legislators (a) to get credit for perceived benefit increases and/or (b) to control costs by reducing real benefit levels under the guise of keeping money benefits the same or rising less than inflation.

If benefits are automatically indexed for inflation, three major technical issues must be addressed:

- The frequency with which adjustments are made
- The program parameters to be indexed
- The price index for the adjustments

INDEXING FREQUENCY

Choosing the frequency of benefit adjustment involves a tradeoff between benefit adequacy and administrative cost. The more frequent the adjustments, the greater the responsiveness of the program to price increases. But each adjustment implies administrative costs, since the adjustments themselves must be developed and information on the adjustments must be disseminated to program staff and incorporated into automated systems.

PARAMETERS TO BE INDEXED

Several different dollar-denominated parameters are used in calculating benefit levels under an assistance program: maximum benefit levels for households with zero net income, deductions, and any ceilings on deductions that are calculated on the basis of expenses. All these parameters must be indexed if full inflation adjustment is to be accomplished.

CHOOSING THE PRICE INDEX

Choosing a price index depends on its intended purpose. For instance, if benefits in an assistance program are meant to be directed to a specific form of consumption, such as food, then a price index that reflects changes in that consumption category is the logical choice. For an income eligibility cutoff limit intended to reflect a household's overall degree of poverty, a more general price index is suitable.

Choosing an appropriate adjustment index also entails deciding whether prices people pay or wages people earn is more appropriate. The objective of ensuring that program recipients can buy a constant amount of real consumption items implies a price index. However, if prices rise faster than average wages, a price index gives assistance program recipients greater protection against inflation than people who have to buy the same goods and services with income they earn. Some observers argue that recipients of public assistance should be afforded only the same amount of protection against price changes that is afforded to the typical worker.[11]

COST-OF-LIVING ADJUSTMENTS IN THE FOOD STAMP PROGRAM

Most of the important features of the Food Stamp Program are adjusted automatically for changes in prices. These indexing features played an important role in maintaining the real value of program benefits during the 1980s, when inflation eroded the real value of many other assistance programs, such as AFDC, to a substantial degree. The Thrifty Food Plan amounts on which maximum program benefits are based are adjusted automatically to reflect changes in food prices each October 1. The standard deduction used to calculate net income is also adjusted each October 1 based on changes in the nonfood items of the Consumer Price Index for urban households. And the poverty levels on which program eligibility is based are adjusted each year on the basis of the Consumer Price Index. The minimum medical cost for claiming a deduction is not indexed, however, nor are the asset limits or the dependent care deduction.

IN-KIND VERSUS CASH BENEFITS

The final design issue in structuring a benefit program is whether benefits should be conferred in the form of "in-kind" benefits linked directly to specific goods and services or whether they should be provided as cash (usually checks).

Food Stamp Program benefits are provided in the form of food coupons that recipients can exchange for the equivalent value of food at participating supermarkets and other food stores. Food coupons constitute an in-kind benefit, since they can be legally used only to buy food.

The Advantages of Coupons

One frequently cited advantage of providing in-kind rather than cash benefits is that, with in-kind benefits, recipient households will consume greater quantities of socially desirable items than they would if benefits were given as cash. This argument suggests that food coupons prompt households to buy more food than they would under a comparable-value cash assistance plan. Different variants of this argument hold that the increased consumption of food is desirable because (1) it makes the households themselves better off or (2) taxpayers and voters prefer that recipient households consume relatively greater quantities of food than other consumption items.

A key premise of this argument for providing Food Stamp Program benefits as food coupons is that coupons do in fact significantly increase food consumption levels more than equivalent cash assistance. This issue is discussed in detail in Chapter V.

A second argument for in-kind benefits is that taxpayers prefer to know that the *actual assistance that they support* is being devoted directly to consumption items that they feel are socially desirable. This argument differs from the first argument discussed above in that, rather than focusing on the *overall effects on spending patterns,* it focuses on *how the benefits themselves are used*—on whether, at a minimum, recipient households are buying food equal in value to their food stamp assistance levels. Food coupons (as long as they are used by recipients) ensure this.

Either of the two arguments discussed above can be used to develop a political argument for in-kind benefits. One variant of this is to view society's welfare as including *both* food stamp recipients *and* the welfare of taxpayers concerned about how the assistance is used. Others focus only on the needs of the low-income assistance recipients, but argue that *political* considerations may favor an in-kind assistance program on the grounds that taxpayers will be more generous in their support if they approve of the form of the benefit. The political importance of in-kind benefits in the Food Stamp Program appears to be substantial, as is discussed in detail in Chapter VII.

The Disadvantages of Coupons

In-kind benefits have at least four disadvantages:

- The constraints they impose on recipient choice
- The potential embarrassment attached to using them
- Their effects on program administrative costs
- The incentive to engage in illegal behavior (by merchants and participants) to avoid the constraints

CONSTRAINTS ON CHOICE

As noted earlier, that in-kind benefits may encourage recipient house-holds to alter their consumption patterns is often cited as an advan-tage of using in-kind benefits. This aspect of in-kind benefits can also be seen as a disadvantage. To the extent that a household itself is best able to assess what it needs and what purchases will make it best off, its welfare is reduced by benefits that restrict its purchases.

POTENTIAL EMBARRASSMENT FROM USING COUPONS

Recipients may be embarrassed by using coupons that mark them as public assistance recipients. Relatively little information is available on how much stigma attaches to food stamp use. One might expect that, as a group, the elderly may be more sensitive to embarrassment factors than most other categories of recipients. However, results of a survey of elderly Food Stamp Program participants undertaken in 1981 (Blanchard et al., 1982) indicate that only one out of five elderly food stamp recipients was embarrassed to use food stamps. The same study also examined why some elderly people choose not to partici-pate in the program, even though they are eligible. The results showed that stigma was not the major reason for nonparticipation among the elderly respondents surveyed. (A more complete discussion of reasons for nonparticipation in the Food Stamp Program is presented in Chapter 3.)

The findings of another survey-based study also indicate that stigma is not a factor for most households (U.S. General Accounting Office, 1988). A national sample of eligible households were asked about their reasons for nonparticipation. Only 14 percent of eligible respondents who had not applied for food stamps cited embarrass-ment as the reason. (These studies and related work are summarized in Allin and Beebout, 1989.)

ADMINISTRATIVE COSTS

A third disadvantage of using in-kind rather than cash benefits is higher administrative costs. America's financial system provides an extremely efficient way to convey purchasing power in the form of checks. Transferring resources in any other form is less efficient (and more expensive).

Several factors underscore this issue as it applies to food stamps. First, distributing the coupons is more expensive than distributing checks. Second, stores, banks, and the Federal Reserve System all incur higher costs to redeem the coupons than to clear checks. Third, storage and related security costs are higher at each stage of the distribution and redemption process than they would be for the equivalent check value.

ILLEGAL BEHAVIOR

In-kind benefits encourage illegal behavior. Selling stamps for cash (trafficking) and using stamps for non-food items are illegal behaviors that are encouraged by the Food Stamp Program's form of benefits. Cashing-out food stamps would automatically eliminate such illegal behavior—but at the cost of giving up the link between benefits and food purchases. Issues related to client and non-client fraud are discussed in Chapter IV.

Distributing Commodities as an Alterative

As noted in Chapter I, the Food Stamp Program replaced an earlier commodities program. Currently, both the Emergency Food Assistance Program and the Special Supplemental Food Program for Women, Infants, and Children (WIC) Program distribute commodities to low-income households.

Although providing Food Stamp Program benefits in the form of commodities would ensure that program recipients received food and would strengthen support for the program by agricultural interests, commodity distribution would greatly exacerbate the difficulties associated with in-kind benefits.[12] First, food handling and storage costs would greatly increase the administrative costs associated with any given level of benefit transfers. Second, the variety of commodities that could feasibly be distributed, even at higher administrative costs, would be quite limited. Thus, needy households would be less likely to apply to the program and those who did would be less likely to obtain a nutritionally balanced diet. Food stamps represent 25 percent or more of the purchasing resources of many food stamp households. It is inconceivable that a commodities distribution program within the American context could make available food supplies to needy families in anything like this amount.

Notes

1. *U.S. Code of Federal Regulations*, Title 7, Subtitle B, Chapter II, Subchapter C, Part 273, Section 273.1.

2. The limit does not apply to households that contain elderly or disabled members. Also, the total deductions can never be less than zero.

3. See U.S. Congress, Senate, Committee on Agriculture, Nutrition and Forestry (1985) for a discussion of the types of expenses meant to be covered under the standard deduction.

4. Somewhat different income limits apply to households that contain an elderly or disabled member who is treated as a separate household. In these cases, only the income of the elderly or disabled member is counted towards the net income screen. However, a gross income cutoff of 165 percent of the poverty level is applied to the full household in which the elderly or disabled member resides.

5. There is a minimum benefit of $10 for one- and two-person households.

6. As of June 1992, the Thrifty Food Plan monthly cost of food at home for a family of 2 adults and 2 young children was $310.20. The corresponding figures for the other three plans were $386.60, $471.20, and $578.50.

7. Attention has been devoted in recent years to exactly how the adjustment should be made for household size. The current adjustment factors are based on 1965 data. Examination of the possibility of updating the adjustment factors (Nelson, Beebout, and Skidmore, 1985) found other equally defensible adjustment methodologies and data sources. However, the various approaches would almost certainly yield results that are different both from the current adjustment factors and from one another, and the authors found no strong conceptual basis for choosing among the different methodologies and data sources.

8. The opposite problem—benefits being reduced to zero before the eligibility cutoff is reached—leads to the somewhat bizarre situation of a household technically eligible for a program but not eligible for any benefits.

9. This tax rate does not apply to households that are already at their maximum benefit level because their net income is zero. It also does not apply to one- and two-person households that are at the $10 benefit level set by statute as the minimum benefit level for such households.

10. Earnings-related benefit reductions in other assistance programs have the effect of reducing countable food stamp income from sources other than earnings, thus partially offsetting the effects of the increased earnings in the food stamp benefit calculation. Suppose, for example, that a food stamp/AFDC recipient earns an extra $100 of income that is taxed at a rate of 67 percent under the AFDC benefit determination formula. AFDC benefits decline by $67. For the Food Stamp Program, unearned income (the AFDC payment in this case) declines by $67, partially offsetting the $100 increase in earnings. The effect is that food stamp gross income rises by $33. However,

because the food stamp earned income deduction rises by $20, net food stamp income rises only by $13, implying a reduction in food stamps of about $4. Thus, the implicit tax rate on earnings is a $67 reduction in AFDC and a $4 reduction in food stamps, or a total benefit reduction of $71—a 71 percent rate.

11. For a more in-depth discussion of this and other issues associated with indexation, see Ross (1991).

12. A more in-depth analysis of the potential advantages and disadvantages of distributing commodities directly to needy households is provided by the U.S. Department of Agriculture, Food and Nutrition Service (March 1983).

Chapter Three

PROGRAM COVERAGE AND BENEFIT ADEQUACY

To assess whether a program is operating efficiently, it is useful to examine how well it meets its general objectives. This chapter draws on detailed information on the operations of the Food Stamp Program and its intended recipient population to assess how well the program meets its objectives in terms of targeting, adequacy of benefits, and access. Assessments of the program along other dimensions, such as preserving work incentives, containing administrative costs, and achieving low error rates, are provided in subsequent chapters.

PROGRAM PARTICIPATION AMONG ELIGIBLE HOUSEHOLDS

Several participation measures are used to evaluate public assistance programs. The *household participation rate* indicates the percentage of households eligible for a program who actually receive its benefits. It thus measures the proportion of potential program recipient units reached by the program. The *individual participation rate* is the participation rate among persons in eligible households. It differs from the household participation rate to the extent that household size differs among participating and nonparticipating households. Finally, the *benefit participation rate* is defined as actual assistance payment outlays divided by the outlays that would be issued if all eligible households participated in the program. It measures the proportion of potential program benefits that are actually delivered to the target population.

Estimating any of these measures of participation requires data on *actual program participants* for the numerator and on *program participants and eligible nonparticipants* for the denominator. For most assistance programs, aggregate program records and reports provide accurate information on the number of participants. However, program data generally do not provide information on households that are eligible for a program but are not participating; broader population surveys are required.

Ongoing national surveys are used to develop estimates of eligibility rates for various public assistance programs. Among the surveys commonly used for this purpose are (1) the Survey of Income and Program Participation, conducted by the U.S. Census Bureau, (2) the Current Population Survey, conducted by the U.S. Census Bureau, and (3) the Panel Study of Income Dynamics, conducted by the Survey Research Center of the University of Michigan.

Since these are multipurpose surveys, they do not collect sufficiently detailed information on household composition, income, assets, and expenditures to allow the complex eligibility and benefit determination rules for any particular program to be replicated fully. Thus, assessing whether the specific households included in these surveys are actually eligible for a particular program often requires assumptions about the timing of reported income receipt, detailed expenditure patterns, and household composition and living arrangements. As a result, estimates of the number of eligible households for specific programs (and thus estimates of participation rates) vary substantially across different studies. The Survey of Income and Program Participation (SIPP) is the most detailed of the available data sources. But even SIPP does not provide sufficient data to fully assess eligibility for most programs.

In addition to providing insufficiently detailed data, national surveys are known to systematically underreport participation. This systematic underreporting reflects both misreporting by some survey respondents and underrepresentation of the low-income population among the respondents who complete interviews.

All this gives rise to an important methodological problem in estimating participation rates. Program data yield a relatively accurate estimate of participants (the numerator) but no estimate of total eligibles (the denominator). Survey data yield estimates of both, but the participant estimates, at least, are known to be biased downward. If this downward bias is due to underrepresentation of the low-income population, it would be present in the estimated eligibles as well, and the resulting estimate of the participation rate might be relatively free of bias. Furthermore, underreporting of income, which is also known to exist in the survey data, can lead to downward biases when participation rates are estimated based entirely on survey data. In light of these factors, we believe that participation rates constructed

Table III.1 ALTERNATIVE ESTIMATES OF FOOD STAMP PROGRAM
PARTICIPATION RATES, 1984

	Household Participation Rate	Individual Participation Rate	Benefit Participation Rate
Basis of Estimates			
Program data on participants divided by survey-based estimates of eligibles[a]	.60	.66	.80
Survey-based estimates of both participants and eligibles[b]	.41	.51	n.a.

a. Based on Doyle and Beebout (1988).
b. Based on U.S. Congressional Budget Office (1988).
n.a.—not available.

using program data in the numerator and survey-based data in the denominator are the most likely to be correct.

Food Stamp Program Participation Rates

Table III.1 compares estimates of 1984 participation rates using program/survey and survey/survey ratios. For the household participation rate (shown in the first column of the table), *program data on actual participants* yield an estimated participation rate of 60 percent, while the *survey estimates of participants* yield an estimated rate of only 41 percent.[1] The discrepancy for the individual participation rate is comparable. Our earlier discussion suggests that the higher participation rate estimates, shown in the first row of the table, may be the more nearly correct. However, even if one accepts our argument supporting the higher participation rate estimates in Table III.1, the overall *household participation rate* is quite low—60 percent. The *benefit participation rate* is much higher, 80 percent, suggesting that the program is more successful at reaching households that need the program the most. Program and SIPP survey data for 1989 indicate that eligibility has risen more rapidly than participation since 1984, with participation rates falling to 56 percent for households and 66 percent for benefits (Trippe and Doyle, 1992).

To put these food stamp household participation rates into perspective, it is useful to compare them with estimated participation rates in other programs. The AFDC household participation for 1984 has been estimated at 82 percent (Ruggles and Michel, 1987). The SSI household participation rate for the elderly has been estimated at

Table III.2 FOOD STAMP HOUSEHOLD PARTICIPATION RATES BY SELECTED
HOUSEHOLD CHARACTERISTICS, 1985

Characteristics	Household Participation Rate (percent)
Total Households	59
Household Contains an Elderly Member	37
Household Contains a Disabled Member	47
One Female Adult Household with Children	75
Multiple-Adult Household with Children	75
Household Has Earnings	37
Household Has UI Income	76
Income as a Percentage of Poverty Threshold	
1% to 50%	93
51% to 100%	67
Over 100%	15
Monthly Benefit Level for Which the Household Is Eligible	
$0 to $50	36
$51 to $100	65
Over $100	81

Source: Doyle (1990).

between 49 (Zedlewski and Meyer, 1989) and 64 percent (Leavitt and Schulz, 1988). The SSI estimates are in the same range as the food stamp estimate, suggesting that nonparticipation is a problem for that program also.

Food stamp participation rates vary substantially for different types of households (Table III.2). For elderly households and households with earnings, rates are below 40 percent. For single female-parent households with children, by contrast, the participation rate is 75 percent. Participation rates also decline substantially as household income increases and benefits fall.

Reasons for Nonparticipation

Why do eligible households not participate in food stamps and other benefit programs? Besides being interesting in its own right, this question is important for policy, since it has implications for program reform to increase access. Seven reasons are potentially important:[2]

- Households do not realize they are eligible.
- Households believe they do not need the benefits.
- Administrative requirements pose obstacles to participation.
- Physical access to offices poses constraints.

■ Households are embarrassed at using the benefits.
■ Households entitled to low benefit amounts sometimes do not bother to apply.
■ Homeless people have trouble meeting the documentation requirements.

PERCEPTIONS OF ELIGIBILITY FOR FOOD STAMPS

At least three surveys conducted during the 1980s asked eligible households who were not participating in the Food Stamp Program about their reasons for nonparticipation. One of these studies involved an overall sample of the food-stamp-eligible population (U.S. Government Accounting Office, 1988). A second was limited to elderly households (Hollonbeck and Ohls, 1984). A third focused on AFDC recipients (Ohls et al., 1986).

Each of these studies found that a large proportion of eligible nonparticipating households were not aware of their eligibility. The GAO study, admittedly an overestimate, put the proportion of eligible nonparticipants unaware of their eligibility at 51 percent. Hollenbeck and Ohls (1984) found 25 percent of the elderly nonparticipant households who were eligible for the program were unaware of their eligibility. Ohls et al. (1986) put the comparable rate for AFDC recipients at 44 percent. Many of the AFDC recipients who were unaware of their eligibility for food stamps were members of "mixed" households, with members who were not receiving AFDC support.

Complex eligibility rules and mistakes by Food Stamp Program staff in processing applications or in responding to requests for information may be a factor in explaining why households are not aware of their eligibility. This hypothesis is supported by program data on "negative actions" generated by the Food Stamp Program quality control system.[3] Based on a review of negative actions (i.e., application denials or case closings), FNS estimated that 7.4 percent of cases with negative actions were in fact eligible for the program when the negative actions were taken. In addition, while no solid evidence on this is available, it is likely that some households may have reductions in income that make them eligible but believe they are ineligible because of information they obtained from program staff before their income dropped.

NO NEED FOR FOOD STAMPS

In the GAO study cited earlier, eligible households who believed they were eligible for food stamps but had not applied were asked

Table III.3 PRINCIPAL REASON THAT ELIGIBLE HOUSEHOLDS WHO THOUGHT
            THEY WERE ELIGIBLE HAD NOT APPLIED (1986 Survey Data)

Reason	Percentage
Didn't Need Benefit or "Never Bothered"	36
Administrative Requirements	17
Problem Related to Physical Access	15
Embarrassment and Related Factors	14
Other, No Answer	18

Source: GAO (1988).

to indicate the principal reason for not applying. As summarized in
Table III.3, more than a third of the households indicated that they
either did not need the benefits or, for some other nonspecific reason,
simply had not sought food stamp assistance. The two other surveys
of nonparticipants cited earlier obtained similar results.

ADMINISTRATIVE REQUIREMENTS AND PROBLEMS WITH
PHYSICAL ACCESS

A third set of deterrents to participation may be administrative
requirements—the time and money costs of traveling to a Food Stamp
Program office to apply for benefits, and the paperwork and reporting
requirements associated with program participation. The data in
Table III.3 suggest that administrative requirements may be a significant deterrent to participation. Seventeen percent of respondents
who believed that they were eligible but had not applied mentioned
administrative issues as their reason for not participating, and
another 15 percent cited problems related to physical access to a
food stamp office.

Available survey data do not address whether the respondents'
perceptions of administrative burdens and problems were accurate.
Some respondents may have believed complying with the administrative requirements was more burdensome than was in fact the case.
However, additional evidence from the U.S. General Accounting
Office (1988) suggests that administrative factors may indeed affect
access to food stamps. Based on reviews of local office procedures
in selected states, the GAO concluded that program accessibility
varies considerably, that some local offices have restricted operating
hours, and that some provide incomplete information on application
procedures when potential applicants first ask for information.

Local food stamp offices also sometimes impose administrative
burdens that are inconsistent with federal regulations, according to

studies conducted by advocacy groups in various parts of the country. Among the problems often mentioned are (1) requiring that applicants make multiple trips to the food stamp office before they are allowed to file a formal application, (2) providing insufficient information on denial notices for applicants to understand why their applications have been rejected, (3) requiring that applicants supply difficult-to-obtain verification material beyond the documentation required by federal regulations, and (4) failing to inform clients who need immediate food stamp assistance that they have a right to expedited processing of their applications. The advocacy group studies vary considerably in their methodological rigor. However, taken together, they attest to widespread administrative barriers to participation.

A recent exploratory study of the food stamp application process in five local offices in two states reached similar conclusions (Bartlett et al., 1992). Its findings suggest that between 9 and 18 percent of the potential applicants who contact a food stamp office to inquire about benefits may be discouraged from applying by some aspect of the application process. Among the factors mentioned were the time and "hassle" involved, the length of the process, long waits at offices, and difficulties obtaining documentation.

The following quotations from a recent focus group discussion with several elderly persons eligible for but were not participating in food stamps illustrate the participation barriers imposed by administrative requirements (Ponza and Wray, 1989):

> "They give you such a hassle when you got to apply for food stamps. You have to have papers from this, papers from that, papers from the other, proof of this, proof of that. Where do you get all of this proof?"

> "I got food stamps for one month, and the second month they had me fill out some papers. There was a couple of things on the paper that I didn't know how to fill out. They told me I had to bring in the paper filled out. And I just gave up."

> "I'm eligible, but it's so much hassle because I can't get around and catch the bus and go like I want to go. I have to catch the lift. Lots of times you call them and you know at a certain time they're way back and you've got to wait, and so it's just too much of a hassle, you know, to put up with all that. And then certain times you got to go back [to the FSP office] and sign up and all that stuff."

EMBARRASSMENT AT USING FOOD STAMPS

Using food coupons to buy groceries means that a household's participation in the Food Stamp Program is evident to storekeepers and other shoppers; the embarrassment of such visibility is enough to prevent about 14 percent of households who think they are eligible from applying, according to data from the surveys cited earlier.

HOMELESSNESS

Homelessness is a significant deterrent to Food Stamp Program participation. Mental health problems, transportation barriers, and problems in acquiring documentation, all contribute. A recent national survey of homeless persons revealed that, although virtually all respondents were eligible, according to their income responses, only 18 percent were receiving food stamps (Burt and Cohen, 1988). The same study also found that many local food stamp offices reported difficulty in determining the eligibility of homeless applicants due to the limited documentation that they can supply.

Legislative changes in 1985, 1987, 1988, and 1990 were designed to reduce the difficulties homeless persons face in obtaining food stamps. These changes include eliminating the requirement for verification of a specific address, providing funding for outreach to the homeless, and allowing the homeless to purchase meals in restaurants. Since several of the measures have gone into effect only recently, the extent to which they succeed in improving access to food stamps for the homeless remains to be seen.

LOW BENEFIT LEVELS

An additional factor that may prompt an eligible household not to participate in the Food Stamp Program, often in conjunction with other factors, is low benefits. As shown earlier in Table III.2, participation rates fall as the benefits to which households are eligible decline. Participation rates are particularly low for the elderly, many of whom are eligible for only the $10 minimum monthly benefit. This is of much less policy concern than other factors limiting participation. These households need benefits less because their incomes are near the cutoff for eligibility.

Policies to Increase Participation

Outreach is one obvious way to increase participation. During the late 1970s, the states were required to engage in active food stamp program outreach activities, such as sponsoring publicity campaigns in the media and providing brochures and posters about the program.

During that period, funding for outreach, like other program administrative costs, was shared by the federal government and the states. In 1981, however, as part of the cost-cutting measures introduced in the early years of the Reagan Administration, the Omnibus Budget Reconciliation Act explicitly prohibited using federal funds for food stamp outreach.

However, increasing concern about hunger led to a provision of the 1987 Stewart B. McKinney Homeless Assistance Act, which allowed federal matching for state funds used to provide information on the Food Stamp Program to the homeless. The following year, the Hunger Prevention Act of 1988 reinstituted the federal matching of outreach expenditures on a more general basis.

Since then, some states and local offices have renewed efforts to increase program participation through publicity programs that inform eligible households about the availability of food stamp benefits. Some of the publicity has been directed at removing the stigma associated with food stamps by characterizing the program as a social insurance entitlement that any eligible household should use freely to support its needs.

Another way to increase participation is to reduce administrative barriers. Current federal regulations contain extensive operational specifications for local offices to do this, by requiring the acceptance of joint applications for food stamp and public assistance programs benefits, and by setting standards for case processing times, due process procedures, and similar administrative matters.[4]

Administrative barriers could be lowered further by providing more help to applicants in meeting paperwork requirements and by reducing documentation and verification standards. However, inevitable tradeoffs appear here too. Increasing staff training and making more staff available to help applicants meet administrative requirements increase program costs. Similarly, imposing more federal standards and increasing federal monitoring of local office practices increase costs and reduce the flexibility of local office operations. Many staff in state and local offices already feel overburdened by what they view as excessive federal regulations in the Food Stamp Program, in comparison to the other public assistance programs they administer.

The inevitable tradeoff between program accessibility and accountability does not help matters. In order to minimize error and fraud, the current program imposes extensive documentation and verification requirements on applicants, burdening clients and deterring participation. Many measures for making the program more accessible, such as reducing verification requirements and reducing the frequency of required recertification interviews, increase administrative error.

Assessing these tradeoffs requires information on the potential increases in participation that could be achieved with particular outreach activities and particular measures to reduce administrative burden, but little solid information is available in this area. In light of the low participation rates and the substantial evidence of barriers to participation described above, such information is of high priority.

THE CHARACTERISTICS OF FOOD STAMP HOUSEHOLDS

The great majority of food stamp households are officially in poverty.[5] Program data for 1991 put the proportion at over 91 percent.[6] Most of the other participants are under 130 percent of poverty.

Demographic Characteristics

Table III.4 shows the demographic characteristics of food stamp participants. The categories are not mutually exclusive (i.e., a family household can contain an elderly person *and* be a single-person household). About 17 percent of food stamp households contain at least one elderly member. Over half these elderly households consist of single elderly persons living alone; most of the remainder are two-person households. Another 9 percent of program households contain a member whom the SSI program defines as disabled and who is younger than 60. As with households that contain an elderly member, the majority of food stamp households that contain disabled persons are either one or two-person households.

Slightly less than one-third of all program households consist of a single person; these households account for 12 percent of participants. Another 61 percent of all food stamp households contain children; these households constitute 82 percent of participants.

Economic Characteristics

As noted in earlier chapters, the Food Stamp Program was never intended to be a comprehensive income maintenance program. Its focus is on helping households attain nutritional adequacy in their diets. Given this, it is not surprising that most Food Stamp Program

Table III.4 CHARACTERISTICS OF HOUSEHOLDS AND PERSONS RECEIVING
FOOD STAMPS, 1991

Selected Characteristics of Households	Percent of Households	Percent of Persons	Average Number of Persons per Household
Demographic Characteristics			
Households That Contain:			
Elderly[a]	16.6	9.4	1.49
Disabled, no elderly[b]	9.2	7.9	2.24
Single person[c]	32.0	12.2	1.00
Children[d]	61.4	81.8	3.50
Single parent with children[e]	40.7	48.1	3.10
Multiple adults with children[f]	17.8	31.6	4.65
Economic Characteristics			
Households That Receive:			
Aid to Families with Dependent Children (AFDC)	40.8	52.2	3.36
Supplemental Security Income (SSI)	19.3	13.3	1.81
General assistance	10.1	6.4	1.67
Social Security income	17.9	12.3	1.80
Earned income	19.8	26.4	3.49
Other income[g]	16.7	18.3	2.87
No income	8.7	6.2	1.88
Total	100.0	100.0	2.6

Source: Summer 1991 Food Stamp Quality Control sample.
a. Households that contain at least one member age 60 or older.
b. Households that receive SSI income but do not contain a member age 60 or older.
c. Households that contain only one member.
d. Households that contain at least one member age 17 or younger.
e. Households that contain only one member age 18 or older and children (at least one member age 17 or younger).
f. Households that contain two or more members age 18 or older and children (at least one member age 17 or younger).
g. Other income includes unemployment income, veteran's benefits, Workers' Compensation, other government benefits, household contributions, household deemed income, household loans, and other unearned income.

households also receive assistance from one or more government cash transfer programs. About 41 percent participate in AFDC, 19 percent participate in SSI, and 10 percent receive support under state or local general assistance. Eighteen percent receive social security.

A significant number of America's poor households include someone who is employed. In some instances, the worker does not work

Figure III.1 FOOD STAMP PROGRAM HOUSEHOLDS, 1980–1991

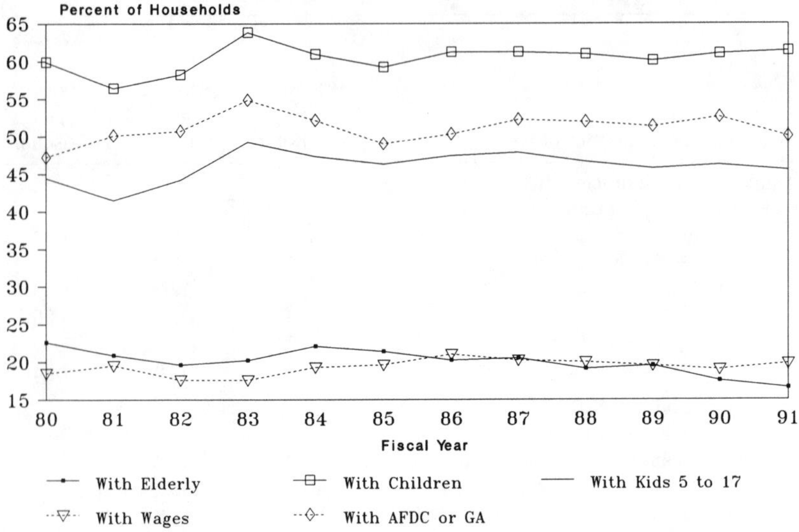

Source: See Appendix Table C.2.

enough hours to be above the poverty line; in other instances, the wage rate is too low to bring them out of poverty even at full-time, full-year work. In the Food Stamp Program, approximately 20 percent of recipient households have income from earnings. These households tend to be larger than the average food stamp household and constitute 26 percent of program participants.

Thus far, the discussion has focused on the characteristics of Food Stamp Program participants in 1988. As shown in Figure III.1, these characteristics are quite stable over time.

Summary

The food stamp household characteristics information presented above can be summarized by identifying the main categories of households which make up the food stamp population. About 41 percent of food stamp households are AFDC families. Another 17 percent are one- or two-person households with an elderly member. The remaining 42 percent are not elderly and are not on AFDC; approximately half of these have children.

FOOD STAMP PARTICIPATION DURING ECONOMIC DOWNTURNS

Less than one-third of the unemployed are covered by unemployment insurance (Corson and Nicholson, 1988). It is therefore desirable that public assistance programs provide help to families who are made poor by economic downturns. How well does the Food Stamp Program function as a countercyclical income cushion?

The confounding effects of program changes make it impossible to identify the exact relationship between unemployment and Food Stamp Program participation.[7] During the recession of the early 1970s, the geographic coverage of the program had recently been expanded. In the 1980 downturn, the effects of eliminating the purchase requirement were still being felt; and during the 1981–1982 recession case loads were influenced by tightened eligibility and benefits determination rules for both food stamps and AFDC. However, program participation rose during each of these recessions and also *declined* in the periods after each recession. This provides substantial evidence that economic factors were important in affecting participation during these periods (for reference, see Chapter I, Figure I.1).

With respect to the most recent economic downturn, participation in the Food Stamp Program began rising in mid-1989, well before the official start of the recession (as measured in national unemployment statistics). The reasons for this 1989 increase in participation are not fully understood. Most of this initial increase was probably due to factors other than the oncoming recession, although the beginning of the recession may have influenced participation in some states (U.S. Department of Agriculture, Food and Nutrition Service, 1990).

During the summer of 1990, the number of unemployed workers nationally began to increase very rapidly. Food stamp participation, after having leveled off during the early and mid part of 1990, began rising very rapidly during the fall of 1990. Most of this later rise in the food stamp caseload can probably be attributed to the recession. As of the current writing in 1992, caseloads have continued to rise and have reached record numbers.

BENEFIT ADEQUACY

The household income measure currently used by the Census Bureau to measure poverty is based solely on cash income. Hence, the Food

Stamp Program has no direct effect on the official estimates of poverty in the United States. Nonetheless, the benefits do help meet the needs of persons in poor households. A key question is how those benefits should be valued relative to cash benefits.

Methods for Valuing Food Stamp Benefits

The U.S. Bureau of the Census (1984) summarizes three alternative methods for valuing in-kind benefits: the market value approach, the recipient or cash value approach, and the poverty budget-share approach. The "market value" represents the cost of the in-kind benefits if purchased in the marketplace. For the Food Stamp Program, the market value is the face value of the coupons. The "recipient value" represents the cash-equivalent value or the amount of cash the average participant would accept in trade for the in-kind benefits. To the extent that program participants would rather have cash than the same market value of an in-kind benefit, the "recipient value" is less than the "market value." The "poverty budget-share" value reflects the amount required by a family or individual at the poverty level to meet its basic requirements for the in-kind good. Of the three concepts, the first—the cost of the in-kind goods if purchased in the marketplace—is by far the easiest to measure. We thus use this valuation method in considering the impact of the Food Stamp Program and other cash assistance programs in meeting the needs of the low-income population.[8] It should be remembered that doing so may somewhat overstate the value of the benefits to the participants. However, the illustrative calculations presented in U.S. Bureau of the Census (1984) suggest that the degree of overvaluation is probably small.

Food Stamp Benefit Levels

The overall monthly food stamp benefit as of 1991 was $162 per month, approximately $61 per household member (Table III.5). Benefits to elderly households, $42 per person, are lower than average because these households have higher average income levels than other food stamp households, primarily because they receive social security. The average benefits of general assistance recipients are relatively high ($73 per person), reflecting their lower incomes.

Given the benefit formula, benefit levels decline as income levels rise. Benefits average $81 per person in households below 51 percent of the poverty level, $26 per person for households between 101 and 130 percent of the poverty level, and $11 per person for the small number of households over 130 percent of the poverty level.

Patterns of Multiple Program Participation

In an important sense, the Food Stamp Program as currently designed and operated is the cornerstone of the U.S. income maintenance system because it is the only public assistance program available to all low-income families and individuals. From this perspective, the effectiveness of government programs at meeting the needs of the low-income population and at reducing poverty depends on whether and how the low-income population is able to combine food stamps with the benefits available from the other programs in the overall income maintenance system.

In order to consider as broad a range of other government programs as possible, much of our discussion of this issue is based on data from the Survey of Income and Program Participation (SIPP). Thus, the estimates of the receipt of income from other programs presented in the accompanying tables may differ slightly from the estimates based on Food Stamp Program data used earlier.

Multiple program participation is the norm for food stamp recipients. As shown in Table III.6, 95 percent of food stamp recipient households also receive benefits from at least one of 16 other programs included in a recent analysis (Long, 1988), nearly 85 percent from at least two others, and more than 40 percent participate in four or more other programs.

Of government programs targeted specifically to low-income households (see Table III.7), the programs most commonly used by food stamp recipients are Medicaid (69 percent of food stamp households), the National School Lunch Program (44 percent), and AFDC (38 percent). Among government social insurance transfer programs not directed specifically toward low-income households, the most common program overlaps with food stamps are the Social Security Program (26 percent of food stamp households) and the Medicare program (23 percent).

The Effectiveness of Multiple Programs at Reducing Poverty

How effective are these benefit combinations at reducing poverty? We address this question for two common measures of poverty reduc-

Table III.5 AVERAGE MONTHLY FOOD STAMP BENEFIT LEVELS AND INCOME AMOUNTS FOR HOUSEHOLDS WITH SELECTED CHARACTERISTICS, 1991

Selected Characteristics of Households	Income per Household	Benefits per Household	Income per Person	Benefits per Person
Demographic Characteristics				
Households That Contain:				
Elderly[a]	$499	$62	$336	$42
Disabled, no elderly[b]	589	94	263	42
Single person[c]	319	64	319	64
Children[d]	545	216	156	62
Single parent with children[e]	476	204	154	66
Multiple adults with children[f]	728	256	157	55
Economic Characteristics				
Households That Receive:				
Aid to Families with Dependent Children (AFDC)	497	215	148	64
Supplemental Security Income (SSI)	537	74	296	41
Household General Assistance	335	122	200	73
Social Security income	543	75	302	42
Earned income	750	181	215	52
Other income[g]	554	161	193	56
No income	0	178	0	95

Gross Income as Percentage of the Poverty Line[h]

50% or Less	237	226	86	81
51% to 100%	592	124	236	50
101% to 130%	913	67	350	26
Over 130%	936	18	600	11
All Households	472	162	180	61

Source: Summer 1991 Food Stamp Quality Control sample.

a. Households that contain at least one member age 60 or older.

b. Households that receive SSI income but do not contain a member age 60 or older.

c. Households that contain only one member.

d. Households that contain at least one member age 17 or younger.

e. Households that contain only one member age 18 or older and children (at least one member age 17 or younger).

f. Households that contain two or more members age 18 or older and children (at least one member age 17 or younger).

g. Other income includes unemployment benefits, veteran's benefits, Worker's Compensation, other government benefits, household contributions, household deemed income, household loans, and other unearned income.

h. The poverty income guidelines for two- and four-person households were $8,420 and $12,700, respectively, during fiscal year 1991.

Table III.6 EXTENT OF MULTIPLE PROGRAM PARTICIPATION BY FOOD STAMP
        HOUSEHOLDS, 1984

Program Combination	Percent of All Food Stamp Households
Food Stamp Program Only	4.9
Food Stamp Program and:	
One program	10.4
Two programs	19.2
Three programs	23.8
Four programs	22.0
Five programs	14.1
Six programs	4.0
Seven or more programs	1.6
Total Sample	100.0

Source: Long (1988).

Table III.7 FREQUENCY OF PROGRAM PARTICIPATION BY FOOD STAMP
        HOUSEHOLDS

Program	Percent of All Food Stamp Households
Needs-Tested Programs	
Aid to Families with Dependent Children	37.9
Supplemental Security Income (SSI)	21.1
General Assistance	11.6
Women and Infant Children Program (WIC)	11.6
National School Lunch Program	43.5
School Breakfast Program	14.1
Medicaid	69.4
Subsidized housing	9.7
Public housing	13.5
Low Income Home Energy Assistance Program	25.3
Social Insurance Programs	
Social Security	25.9
Unemployment Insurance	3.1
Workers' Compensation	0.5
Veterans' Compensation/Pension	4.2
Railroad Retirement	0.2
Medicare	23.3

Source: Long (1988).

tion: (1) the extent to which food stamp benefits, when added to other income sources, provide Food Stamp Program participants with total purchasing power in excess of the poverty thresholds, and (2) the effectiveness of food stamps and other assistance programs at closing the "poverty gap" between available resources and the resources that would be required to help all households escape poverty. For this discussion we return to program data, as the most accurate source for identifying food stamp households.

Figure III.2 and Appendix Table C.3 show information on the percentage of Food Stamp Program households that are above the poverty threshold when only nonassistance income such as earnings is considered (the bottom part of the bars), when cash assistance and social security income are added in (the middle part of the bars), and when the monetary value of food stamp benefits is added in (the top part of the bars). Only about 3 percent of food stamp households receive nonassistance income that exceeds the poverty limits. When the receipt of cash assistance from government transfer programs is added in, approximately 9 percent of food stamp program households are above the poverty level. Adding in food stamps raises the percentage of food stamp households above poverty to about 16 percent.

Even though program records may somewhat underestimate the number of food stamp households above poverty, it is clear that neither the Food Stamp Program by itself nor the overall set of government assistance programs raises many food stamp households out of poverty.

Figure III.3 displays program data on the size of the poverty gap for various categories of food stamp recipients (see also Appendix Table C.4). The lower portion of the bars in the figure show the income received by food stamp households from sources other than government transfer programs. As indicated in the first segment of the table, the nontransfer income available to the average food stamp household is only 16 percent of the poverty threshold. As shown in the middle segment of the bar in the diagram, public cash assistance programs bring the average household's cash receipts up to 60 percent of the poverty threshold. The top portion of the bar shows that the monetary value of food stamp benefits reduces the poverty gap by an additional 18 percentage points, bringing the total resources available to the average food stamp household up to approximately 78 percent of the poverty level. Thus, while the available assistance programs, including the Food Stamp Program, do not allow the typical food stamp household to escape poverty, they significantly reduce

Figure III.2 INCREMENTAL IMPACT ON THE PERCENTAGE OF FOOD STAMP
HOUSEHOLDS ABOVE POVERTY LINE FROM NON-ASSISTANCE
INCOME, CASH ASSISTANCE INCOME, AND FOOD STAMPS (1991)

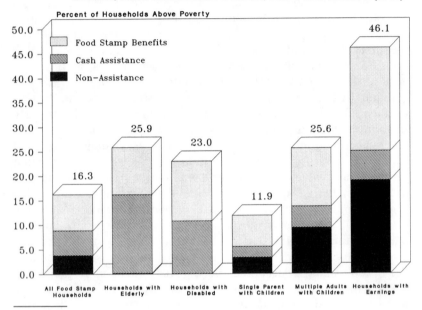

Source: Summer 1991 Food Stamp Quality Control Sample. See Appendix Table C.3.

the gap between the households' resources and the poverty
threshold.[9]

In using the above data to assess the adequacy of Food Stamp
Program benefit levels, it is useful to note that there is an interconnec-
tion through the political process between the AFDC and Food Stamp
Programs, and this interaction may complicate using food stamp
policy, by itself, to reduce poverty. Many states specifically take food
stamp levels into account when determining AFDC levels. States
with very low AFDC levels essentially depend on food stamps to
play a major role in providing needed purchasing power to their
welfare clients. Also, some states may perceive that, because of the
availability of food stamps or because of increases in food stamp
levels, they are justified in reducing AFDC levels or in letting the
real value of AFDC levels slip due to inflation (see Moffitt, 1990).
This political interaction between AFDC and food stamps implies
that attempts to reduce poverty through raising food stamp benefits
may be partially thwarted by offsetting changes in AFDC benefits.

Figure III.3 INCREMENTAL POVERTY GAP REDUCTION FOR FOOD STAMP
HOUSEHOLDS FROM NON-ASSISTANCE INCOME, CASH ASSIS-
TANCE, AND FOOD STAMPS (1991)

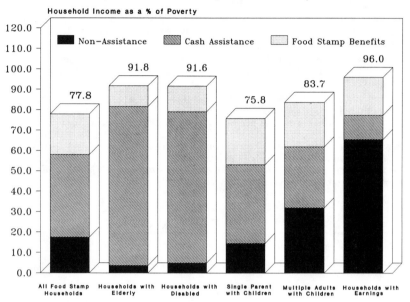

Source: Summer 1991 Food Stamp Quality Control Sample. See Appendix Table C.4.

Notes

1. Two other estimates of Food Stamp Program participation rates have also recently
been published. U.S. General Accounting Office (1988) presents estimates based on
the University of Michigan Panel Study of Income Dynamics, which, in general, are
comparable to those in the second row of the table. However, this GAO study is based
on annual data and requires more assumptions than do studies based on SIPP-based
monthly data. Indeed, the GAO report specifically notes that "our estimate of participation rates based on annual data may be underestimated." This assessment is corrobo-
rated in Trippe (1989). An additional study, Brown (1988), used data from the Consumer Expenditure Survey, and found a much lower household participation rate, 28
percent. However, the estimate of the total number of participants implicit in this latter
study suggests that program participation is severely underreported in the Consumer
Expenditure Survey data set.

2. Allin and Beebout (1989) present additional discussion of the characteristics of
nonparticipating households and their reasons for nonparticipation.

3. U.S. Department of Agriculture, Food and Nutrition Service. "Quality Control
Annual Report, Food Stamp Program, Fiscal Year 1989" (1990).

4. *U.S. Code of Federal Regulations*, Title 7, Subtitle B, Chapter II, Subchapter C,
Part 273, Sections 273.2(g) and 273.15.

5. The poverty guidelines for two- and four-person households were $8,880 and
$13,400, respectively, for 1991.

6. CPS data puts the percentage of food stamp households below poverty at 73 percent. Differences in accounting periods and recipient unit definitions account for part of the discrepancy, and income underreporting in the program data probably account for the rest (see Appendix A for details).

7. An Urban Institute (1985) study discusses the difficulties of developing an econometric model that shows the impacts of the macro economy on Food Stamp Program participation.

8. For an in-depth discussion of other issues associated with evaluating noncash benefits and their impact on poverty, see U.S. Bureau of the Census (1984). Also see Ruggles (1990).

9. Similar conclusions are reached in a recent U.S. Census analysis using 1990 data. For households in poverty and receiving only food stamps, government cash transfers reduced this difference by 36 percent in 1990, while government noncash transfers reduced it 22 percent further. Similarly, the average poverty gap for households in poverty and receiving both food stamps and cash assistance was reduced by 40 percent due to government cash transfers and by an additional 24 percent due to government noncash transfers (U.S. Bureau of the Census, "Measuring the Effect of Benefits and Taxes on Income and Poverty: 1990," August 1991).

Chapter Four

PROGRAM ADMINISTRATION

How an income assistance program is administered has direct impacts on the policy tradeoffs highlighted earlier. For instance, defining program regulations at the federal level of government can help ensure that national targeting goals are met. But federal administration increases costs and inefficiencies due to difficulties in adjusting for justifiable differences in local conditions. Similarly, program errors can be reduced by requiring households to supply extensive documentation of income and other household circumstances, but this reduces effective access to the program by those entitled to its services. Costs can be reduced by lowering administrative staff, but this increases program errors and reduces access.

LEVEL OF FUNCTIONAL RESPONSIBILITY

An important set of decisions in designing the administrative structure of a public assistance program involves what levels of government should perform various administrative functions. Uniform operational procedures consistent with national objectives argue for federal control. In addition, federal administration can reap economies of scale in certain administrative functions. In particular, under federal administration, development of program rules and regulations, such as rules for defining income or rules for defining household composition, can be done by a single entity. If these responsibilities are assigned to sub-federal levels of government, the effort must be duplicated in multiple jurisdictions, which may not only cause considerable inequity across jurisdictions but also create incentives for program participants to move from one jurisdiction to another.

Counterbalancing these advantages of federal administration, however, are important potential problems concerning responsiveness to local conditions. There are major differences across the United States in costs of living, population densities, and labor market conditions, and these factors may affect how program operations can most effectively and efficiently be organized. If administration is federalized, it may be very difficult practically, and impossible politically, to develop national regulations that can efficiently accommodate different local conditions and need.

In addition, though federal administration can reap certain economies of scale, it can work against efficiency along other dimensions. If a program is administered federally, for example, legal standards of equity require that program rules be interpreted consistently throughout the country. However, this means that questions of regulatory interpretation must be "filtered up" to national decision makers and then "filtered back down" to local offices, incurring major time and budget costs. Administration carried out at the federal level also necessitates extremely complex regulations and procedural manuals to accommodate the many differences in local conditions discussed above.[1]

Administration of the Food Stamp Program

Responsibility for administering the Food Stamp Program is shared between federal, state, and, in some cases, local governments. In order to ensure that federal goals for the program are achieved, the federal government, through the Food and Nutrition Service (FNS) of the U.S. Department of Agriculture, develops and disseminates detailed regulations specifying requirements for how the program should be operated. Within FNS, there are two layers of administration. Overall policy and regulations are developed nationally at FNS's central offices in Alexandria, Virginia, just outside of Washington, DC. FNS also maintains 7 regional offices which disseminate information about program regulations to the states in their regions, monitor state performance, and provide technical assistance.

Actual responsibility for determining how the federal regulations are implemented and for day-to-day program operations rests with state governments or, at the states' discretion, with local governments (usually counties). In the states that have chosen to operate the program at the local level, state officials perform liaison functions between the federal and local governments, such as overseeing local operations and assembling information about local operations to meet state-level reporting requirements specified by FNS. In most areas, the same offices (and usually the same workers) who administer food stamps also administer other public assistance programs, including, most importantly, AFDC, general assistance, and Medicaid.

The Food Stamp Program's detailed federal regulations and federal accountability requirements are seen by the staffs of these local offices as a considerable and unnecessary burden. This is particularly the case when the federal requirements are changed frequently. The argument is that, while basic federal standards are appropriate, detailed and frequently changing federal regulations—for a program administered by state and local officials with their own accountability mechanisms—can hinder rather than help the program in meeting its cost-control goals.

Monitoring Program Performance

Several measures of program error rates are commonly used in monitoring public assistance programs. These include:

- The percentage of cases with overpayments (including both eligible participants whose benefits are too high and ineligible cases receiving benefits to which they are not entitled)
- The percentage of cases with underpayments
- The percentage of denials and terminations (negative actions) where the households were, in fact, eligible for benefits
- Overpayments as a percentage of the total dollars of benefits issued
- Underpayments as a percentage of the total dollars of benefits issued

The accounting systems and other program records used in ongoing administration of a program do not contain enough data to estimate program error rates. As a result, in order to obtain this information, it is necessary to conduct reviews or audits. In many public assistance programs, these reviews, which are often called "quality control" or QC reviews, typically involve reviewing the case files, reinterviewing clients, and rechecking verification materials.

Error Rates in the Food Stamp Program

The Food Stamp Program requires all states to conduct periodic QC reviews of samples of their food stamp cases. During these reviews, specially trained workers examine the written case files, reinterview clients, recheck verification sources, and check the accuracy of the calculations made in determining program eligibility and benefits. Federal staff workers then re-review a sample of the state review cases, and the results of these re-reviews are used to adjust the state-determined error rates for any inconsistencies in the accuracy of the review process across states. The number of state reviews per year varies from about 600 to 3,000 per state, with larger states tending to have larger samples.[2]

As shown in Table IV.1, about 8.4 percent of food stamp cases are estimated to have underissuance errors, and 15.5 percent involve overissuances or issuances to ineligibles. However, the dollar error rates as a percentage of total benefit outlays are considerably lower: 2.5 percent for underissuances and 7.4 percent for overissuances. In addition, approximately 6.0 percent of negative actions—i.e., either terminations or denials—are estimated to be incorrect.

In terms of dollars, $763 million of food stamp benefits were issued as benefits in FY 1988 in excess of the amounts clients were entitled to, thus benefiting the clients incorrectly. About $260 million were incorrectly withheld from client benefits. In addition, there were substantial numbers of incorrect denials of benefits, the dollar value of which is not calculated.

Policy Issues

The substantial error levels in administering food stamps have been an important focus of public policy discussions over the past 15 years. When error rates were first systematically measured in the mid 1970s, overissuance rates were found to be well above 10 percent. Concern about these levels led to federal legislative actions that created financial incentives for states to lower error rates and imposed fiscal sanctions on states with rates exceeding federally specified standards.

These standards became successively more stringent over time until, by fiscal year 1985, all states were subject to a 5 percent maximum error rate tolerance level for overpayments. Most states had error rates substantially in excess of that figure and became subject to sanctions. By October 1985, $339 million of sanctions had been assessed on 50 states.[3]

There is little doubt that the fiscal sanctions system contributed to the reduction in overpayment error rates during the 1980s (Table IV.2). Faced with these fiscal threats, states took a variety of steps to improve accuracy, including: increased case documentation requirements; increased case reviews by supervisory personnel; computer

Table IV.1 FOOD STAMP PROGRAM ERROR RATES (Fiscal Year 1988)

	Case Errors			Dollar Errors		
	Average Number of Food Stamp Cases per Month (In thousands)	Estimated Error Rate	Esitmated Number of Cases in Error per Month	Annual Dollars of Food Stamp Benefits Issued (Millions of dollars)	Estimated Error Rate	Estimated Annual Dollars of Benefits in Error (Millions of dollars)
Underissuances	6,648,980	8.42 %	559,844	$10,283	2.53 %	$260
Overpayments and Payments to Ineligibles	6,648,980	15.47	1,028,597	$10,283	7.42	$763
Total[a]	6,648,980	23.89	1,588,441	$10,283	9.95	$1,023

Source: U.S. Department of Agriculture, Food and Nutrition Service, "Quality Control Annual Report, Food Stamp Program, Fiscal Year 1988," September 1990.

NA = Not applicable.

a. Total excludes termination and denial errors, for which dollar estimates are not available.

Table IV.2 FOOD STAMP DOLLAR ERROR RATES OVER TIME
(Percent of Total Benefits Issued)

Period	Overpayments	Underpayments	Total
Jan.–Dec. 1975	15.8	1.9	17.7
Jan.–Dec. 1976	13.0	1.9	14.9
Jan.–Dec. 1977	11.9	2.2	14.1
Oct. 1980–Sept. 1981	9.9	2.5	12.4
Oct. 1981–Sept. 1982	9.5	2.4	12.0
Oct. 1982–Sept. 1983	8.3	2.4	10.9
Oct. 1983–Sept. 1984	8.6	2.3	10.9
Oct. 1984–Sept. 1985	8.3	2.2	10.5
Oct. 1985–Sept. 1986	8.1	2.3	10.4
Oct. 1986–Sept. 1987	7.6	2.7	10.3
Oct. 1987–Sept. 1988	7.4	2.5	9.9
Oct. 1988–Sept. 1989	7.2	2.5	9.8
Oct. 1989–Sept. 1990	7.4	2.5	9.8

Source: Data supplied by U.S. Department of Agriculture, Food and Nutrition Service.

matching of client case file data against other sources of financial information, such as earnings data maintained by states for administering the UI program; and development of "error prone profiles" to focus error control activities on cases which, based on their characteristics, have particularly high probabilities of error.

However, as these techniques were increasingly implemented, many state and local Food Stamp Program staff members began complaining that the emphasis of the system on overpayment errors (as opposed to underpayment errors) was leading workers to be too conservative in granting benefits, and that the extensive time required for repeated case checking was diverting resources from providing needed services to program applicants and participants. Faced with increasing protests by the states, which argued that they were being held to unattainable standards, Congress enacted legislation in 1985 that essentially placed a moratorium on the collection of additional sanctions (most of which had not been paid pending actions initiated by the states) and requested that two reports on the Food Stamp Program QC system be prepared, one by the National Academy of Sciences and one by FNS.

Those reports were completed in 1987 (Affholter and Kramer, ed., 1987; U.S. Department of Agriculture, Food and Nutrition Service, 1987). In 1988, partially on the basis of those studies, legislation was passed that included underpayments as well as overpayments in the financial incentive structure facing the states.

The 1988 legislation also altered the error rate standards in ways that made fewer states subject to sanctions. In particular, a three-tier system was set up, under which: (1) states with net error rates below 6 percent receive financial incentives, based on the degree to which they are under this threshold; (2) states with net error rates above an upper tolerance level are liable for all overissuances above that rate; and (3) states with net error rates between 6 percent and the upper tolerance level have no financial rewards or penalties. The upper tolerance rate used in assessing penalties is computed as one percentage point above the lowest historical average rate.

Possibilities for Future Error Reduction

At some point, the costs of further error reduction outweigh the possible benefits. The nature of the program makes considerable error inevitable. As described in earlier chapters, in order to target program benefits effectively for example, the Food Stamp Program has evolved a highly complex set of regulations concerning eligibility and benefit determination. These regulations require that households supply, and that program staff process accurately, very detailed information on household composition, income sources, assets, shelter expenses, and other circumstances. Furthermore, these complex program rules are frequently changing as new food stamp legislation is passed.

Nevertheless, evidence based on cross-state variation in error rates suggests that further reduction in error rates may be reasonably attainable in some states. Table IV.3 shows error rates for states divided into quintiles on the basis of error rates. For instance, the first panel of the table shows the error rates for the 20 percent of states with the highest error rates, the second panel shows the error rates for the next highest 20 percent of states, etc. These data demonstrate substantial variation in error rates across states, with the high-error states having an average error of 12.2 percent—more than twice the average error rate in the 20 percent of states with the lowest errors.

Even if we ignore the bottom quintile on the grounds that most of the states in it are not representative, the variation across the remaining four quintiles encompasses nearly 4 percentage points of error. The previously mentioned study conducted by FNS in 1987, which also examined the feasibility of statistically adjusting state error rates for differences in caseload characteristics, found substantial variation in state error rates, even after adjusting for differences in state caseload characteristics.[4] This implies that there are influences, other than caseload differences, that substantially affect program error rates. While there is little information about what these influences

Table IV.3 PERCENTAGE DOLLAR ERROR RATES BY STATE (Fiscal Year 1988)

State	Error Rate[a]
Highest Quintile	
District of Columbia	14.57
South Carolina	13.69
New York	12.86
Oklahoma	12.28
Tennessee	12.12
California	11.75
Indiana	11.37
Massachusetts	11.30
Wisconsin	10.96
Alaska	10.83
Quintile Average	12.17
Second Highest Quintile	
Georgia	10.80
Ohio	10.78
Iowa	10.64
Illinois	10.52
Idaho	10.45
West Virginia	10.38
Washington	10.27
Texas	10.25
Oregon	9.98
Alabama	9.86
Quintile Average	10.39
Middle Quintile	
Arizona	9.85
Louisiana	9.80
New Mexico	9.68
Florida	9.37
North Carolina	9.14
Rhode Island	9.08
Vermont	9.03
Nebraska	8.87
Pennsylvania	8.67
Missouri	8.66
Quintile Average	
	9.22
Second Lowest Quintile	
Minnesota	8.65
Maryland	8.62
Delaware	8.54
Colorado	8.51

Second Lowest Quintile (continued)

Michigan	8.33
Utah	8.22
Mississippi	8.07
New Hampshire	7.77
Connecticut	7.68
Wyoming	7.64
Quintile Average	8.20

Lowest Quintile

New Jersey	7.57
Virginia	7.45
Maine	7.42
Kansas	6.21
Montana	5.90
Kentucky	5.48
Arkansas	5.44
North Dakota	5.41
Hawaii	5.34
South Dakota	4.45
Nevada	2.69
Quantile Average	5.76

Source: U.S. Department of Agriculture, Food and Nutrition Service, "Quality Control Annual Report, Food Stamp Program, Fiscal Year 1990." September 1991.
a. Includes both underpayments and overpayments.

are,[5] we believe the quality of state and local administration is an important factor. This suggests considerable additional room for error reduction among the high-error states, while still keeping costs at reasonable levels.

ADMINISTRATIVE COSTS

A second key indicator of administrative performance in a public assistance program is the costs of program operations. The more efficiently a program is administered, the higher the proportion of total program expenditures that goes as benefits to the target population, other things equal.

Many different types of costs are involved in administering a public assistance program. Since public assistance is essentially a service-oriented function, the bulk of program expenditures tend to be for staff salaries and related fringe benefits. However, office space, equipment, supplies, data processing, and other components are also important.

In general, the only cost data available for a program are the data generated by the government accounting systems that monitor costs for purposes of fiscal reporting and accountability. One difficulty of this from the point of view of policy analysis is that accounting systems tend to track costs *by line item* rather than *by function*, making it difficult or impossible to assess the potential impacts on costs of alternative policy changes.

For instance, it is relatively easy to determine how many case workers there are working in an assistance program, but not how much of their time is being spent performing eligibility calculations that might be eliminated by a proposed policy simplification. It is this latter information that is important for policy analysis. Policy analysts are usually forced to do the best they can with aggregate accounting data. Occasionally, however, cost data are collected separately from the accounting process to evaluate a particular program innovation, such as a change in eligibility and benefit determination processes or a change in food stamp issuance methods.

Administrative Costs in the Food Stamp Program

All benefit outlay costs in the Food Stamp Program are borne by the federal government; administrative costs are assumed jointly by the federal government and the states. For most administrative cost categories, these costs are shared equally between the federal and state governments. However, the federal government pays a greater share of administrative costs in certain areas, including computer system development, fraud control, and employment and training activities, which Congress has particularly encouraged.

That Food Stamp Program benefit outlay costs are borne by the federal government probably contributes to high program error rates, because the state and local governmental entities responsible for administering the program do not directly bear the fiscal costs (in terms of higher benefit outlays) that result from errors. This impetus is further exacerbated because states are required to bear half the costs of program administration. It has been argued that this cost structure creates incentives for states to devote too few resources to program administration, since the expenditure of additional administrative resources increases state costs while any resultant savings in reduced errors accrue only to the federal government. The federal

Table IV.4 FOOD STAMP PROGRAM ADMINISTRATIVE COSTS
(Fiscal Year 1988) (In millions of dollars)

	Federal	Non-Federal	Total
Certification	$625	$624	$1,249
Issuance	76	76	152
ADP-Related[a]	79	68	147
Employment and Training	101	46	147
Other	337	240	577
Total	$1,218	$1,054	$2,272

Source: Data supplied by U.S. Department of Agriculture, Food and Nutrition Service.
a. Some ADP costs may be included in other categories.

QC system sanctions described earlier counterbalance these incentives by applying direct financial sanctions for high error rates.

Because state Food Stamp Program administrative costs are partially matched by the federal government, the states are required to develop detailed plans for tracking program costs and for allocating joint and indirect costs between food stamp-related activities and other programs. These plans are subject to approval by the U.S. Food and Nutrition Service, the federal agency responsible for the program. The states then file periodic cost reports based on these plans with the federal government, using a reporting form requiring costs to be broken down by major functional category.

As shown in Table IV.4, the total administrative costs of the Food Stamp Program, including the employment and training component, were more than $2.2 billion in Fiscal Year 1988. This figure was about 17 percent of total state and federal outlays on the program. The federal share of administrative costs was $1.2 billion, approximately 9 percent of federal program outlays. For the AFDC program in 1988, by comparison, federal and state administrative costs together constituted 12 percent of total costs, with the federal government assuming approximately half of this total.[6]

The single largest functional category of costs is certification costs, which includes the staff costs associated with determining and periodically reviewing eligibility and benefits (Table IV.4). Other important categories include issuance costs, employment and training costs, and costs related to computer processing.

Administrative Efficiency in the Food Stamp Program

Annual administrative costs per food stamp case vary substantially by state, from an average of $108 per case in the 10 states with the lowest costs to well in excess of $200 in the high-cost states (Table IV.5). This wide cross-state variation in Food Stamp Program administrative costs has frequently been interpreted as evidence that program operating efficiency could be increased in some states. However, it has also been argued that much or all of the variation is due to factors beyond states' control, such as regional differences in wage levels and differences in the characteristics of cases in different states' caseloads.[7]

Hamilton, et al. (1989) concluded that both efficiency and unavoidable regional differences play a role. They found that variation in factors beyond states' control accounted for about one-third of total observed cross-state cost variation, and that, based on such factors, high cost states might be expected to have costs approximately 70 percent higher than low cost states. However, the differences between low-cost and high-cost states in Table IV.5 are considerably greater than this, suggesting that there is room for efficiency gains in high-cost states.

This raises the issue of whether the federal government should develop a "performance standards" system that would create incentives for states to have low costs (and/or penalties for high ones). Prior to the Hamilton, et al. study, it was not clear whether it was possible to estimate adjustment factors for conditions beyond the states' control. Hamilton, et al. conclude that creating such a system would be feasible; however, to date no policy initiatives in this direction have been undertaken.

Developing a set of performance standards would be a relatively complex process, even if technically feasible. And if the standards had real "teeth" in them (in the form of significant fiscal sanctions for high cost states), the process of developing and implementing such standards would inevitably become highly politicized because of the amounts of matching fund money involved. Based on the experience of the federal government in attempting to implement what was essentially a performance standards system with regard to QC error rates in the 1980s, and given the technical ambiguities involved in making adjustments for caseload characteristics, we judge that implementing a performance standards system based on administrative costs would be politically difficult if not impossible. Enormous amounts of both federal and state resources could be spent developing and arguing about a system which in the end would probably not get implemented for political reasons. In light of this, the government's implicit decision not to follow-up further on the Hamilton et al. study is, we believe, a sound one.

Table IV.5 FOOD STAMP PROGRAM ADMINISTRATIVE COSTS PER CASE, BY
STATE (Fiscal Year 1988)

State	Annual Administrative Cost Per Case
Highest Quintile	
Alaska	$522
Arizona	276
New Jersey	272
Massachusetts	247
Delaware	238
Wyoming	230
Montana	223
California	219
Connecticut	219
Georgia	218
Quintile Average	266
	($238 without Alaska)
Second Highest Quintile	
District of Columbia	214
New Hampshire	208
Rhode Island	204
Utah	197
New Mexico	195
South Carolina	194
South Dakota	193
Idaho	192
Hawaii	190
New York	187
Quintile Average	198
Middle Quintile	
Nevada	184
Maryland	183
Indiana	178
Vermont	177
Virginia	177
Kansas	177
North Dakota	167
North Carolina	162
Washington	161
Texas	160
Quintile Average	173
Second Lowest Quintile	
Florida	159
Missouri	149
Pennsylvania	145

continued

Table IV.5 FOOD STAMP PROGRAM ADMINISTRATIVE COSTS PER CASE, BY
          STATE (Fiscal Year 1988) (continued)

State	Annual Administrative Cost Per Case
Second Lowest Quintile (continued)	
Kentucky	145
Iowa	145
Alabama	144
Minnesota	142
Arkansas	140
Oregon	137
Oklahoma	136
Quintile Average	144
Lowest Quintile	
Illinois	130
Wisconsin	126
Maine	125
Nebraska	120
Tennessee	119
Colorado	112
Michigan	108
Louisiana	100
Mississippi	100
Ohio	90
West Virginia	63
Quintile Average	108

Source: U.S. Department of Agriculture, Food and Nutrition Service, "Food Stamp
Program Information for FY 1980 through FY 1990," July 1991.

Obtaining Cost Reductions through Reductions in Performance on Other Objectives

If administrative cost reductions cannot be achieved through direct
efficiency gains, what about achieving them by accepting reduced
program performance on other dimensions? In order to provide a
basis for making these political choices, it is important to quantify
the relevant tradeoffs as accurately as possible. Key questions are:
To what degree would targeting objectives have to be given up in
order to simplify the program enough to significantly reduce administrative costs? To what degree would a reduction in the resources
allocated to administering the program increase program error rates?
We address these questions using the relatively little information
available, all of which came from cost information compiled for
specific studies.

Administrative cost savings through program simplification are often directly related to reduced target efficiency. In a demonstration involving alternative forms of program simplification which were tested in several states during the 1980s (Ohls, et al., 1986), the state in the demonstration with the greatest gains in simplification was able to achieve reductions in administrative costs in the range of 6 percent. However, these cost gains came at the cost of a considerable reduction on benefit targeting. Client benefit levels (and thus the success of the program in meeting its targeting objectives) were affected[8] for approximately half the caseload, and some of the effects were substantial.

A second state was able to hold targeting effects down to lower levels, with fewer than 10 percent of the food stamp caseload being affected by benefit changes. However, administrative cost savings were correspondingly smaller—in the range of one to two percent. Two other sites implemented simplification plans that had much smaller effects on the client benefits, but these changes had no detectable effects on costs.[9]

POSSIBLE COST REDUCTIONS FROM REDUCING LINKS BETWEEN PROGRAM BENEFITS AND FOOD PURCHASES

As noted, issuing food stamp benefits requires higher administrative costs than needed for a direct cash program of the same magnitude. Evidence on the size of this tradeoff for the Food Stamp Program was obtained in a study of the effects of a demonstration program that cashed out food stamps for elderly recipients in eight sites throughout the country (Blanchard, et al., 1982). Savings in issuance costs of about 38 percent were estimated to be possible by switching away from the coupon-based issuance system at the eight sites. A recent study of the effects of a demonstration cashout program in selected counties in Alabama concluded that issuance costs could be cut in half in those counties by issuing program benefits as checks rather than coupons (Fraker, et al., 1992).

OTHER ADMINISTRATIVE PERFORMANCE INDICATORS

A third important aspect of administrative performance is the *quality* of services provided. Key quality issues include whether program offices are easily accessible to clients, whether clients are treated courteously, how quickly applications are processed, whether program staff provide sufficient information to allow clients to file accurate and timely applications, and whether clients are referred to other support services they may need in addition to benefits.

The only quality aspect that is usually measured is the timeliness with which applications are processed. Many offices have automatic systems that track information about cases in the application process. Even for offices that do not have automated data on application processing times, timeliness usually can be relatively easily measured from manual case reviews, since both the beginning of the application process (submission of the application) and the disposition of the application are reflected in dated hard copy documents contained in the case file.

Food stamp regulations require that all applications be processed within 30 days, as long as the applicant supplies timely documentation and other information needed to process the application. Furthermore, processing of applications from "expedited" cases—those that have no resources to obtain food—is required within 5 days.

According to the most recent comprehensive study of timeliness, which used detailed case record data and interviews with program staff, the average processing time was 20 days for regular food stamp applications, and 7 days for expedited processing, with the 5 day processing requirement being met for only 60 percent of the households (Esrov and SRA Technologies, 1987). The same study found the error rate for issuing benefits within the expedited services program to be 6 percent, slightly lower than the 7 percent error rate in the regular food stamp program. That study also examined error rates of the procedures used in screening applicants to identify cases for expedited processing, finding that 16 percent of the households processed through the regular food stamp program channels should have been directed to apply for expedited services.

ADMINISTERING THE COUPON ISSUANCE AND REDEMPTION PROCESSES

The administrative issues discussed so far in this chapter apply to most public assistance programs. This section discusses three key aspects of program administration that are unique to the Food Stamp Program because of the nature of the benefit: issuance procedures, coupon redemption by the Federal Reserve System, and monitoring retailer compliance with program regulations.

Issuance of Benefits

Several methods of issuing food stamp benefits are currently in use. In some parts of the country, food coupons are mailed directly to recipient households. In others, households are issued "authorization to participate" (ATP) cards and use those cards to obtain food coupons at issuance locations. These may, depending on the area, be local food stamp offices or private business establishments such as banks, stores, or check-cashing agencies. Still other areas have direct, in-person issuance, without ATP cards. And in some areas, food stamp offices mail coupons to some households and have direct delivery or ATP-based systems for others, depending on household circumstances and address.

Mail issuance is more convenient for clients than direct delivery or ATP systems, because the latter two methods require travel to a special location to pick-up benefits. However, the latter systems avoid loss or theft of coupons in the postal system. They also reduce fraud by requiring clients to produce identification and acknowledge benefit receipt.

In recent years, various forms of electronic benefits transfer (EBT) have been tried for food stamp benefit issuance, under which program participants' food stamp benefit accounts are electronically debited when they purchase food. In principle, EBT is the perfect system. It minimizes inconvenience, stigma, fraud, and coupon misuse without severing the link between benefits and food purchases. The most thoroughly tested EBT system to date involves a program in Reading, Pennsylvania, which began as a demonstration in 1984. For the 3,400 clients participating in the demonstration, food stamp benefits took the form of computer-based accounts based at a central EBT center. Clients buying food at a designated retail outlet presented photo identification cards coded with food stamp account numbers. Store checkout clerks then debited the accounts by the food purchase amounts, using remote terminals linked to the central computer via telephone.[10]

The Reading demonstration proved the feasibility of EBT. Both clients and retail outlets were enthusiastic about its convenience, and the demonstration procedures suffered less from benefit losses and diversions than did the ATP-based system used as a comparison. However, at least at the scale of the Reading project, EBT was substantially more expensive than conventional issuance methods. Additional EBT tests are underway or planned in several locations with a variety of transfer technologies, and legislation passed in 1990 authorized states to use EBT systems on a permanent basis, *if* the states can demonstrate no increase in issuance costs.

Overseeing the Coupon Supply and Coupon Redemption Processes

Although coupon issuance to clients is the responsibility of the state and local governments operating the program, the federal government is responsible for supplying the coupons and for redeeming them through the banking system. Figure IV.1 provides an overview of coupon flows through the system.

The coupons are printed by the American Bank Note Company in Horsham, Pennsylvania and Bedford Park, Illinois. The printed coupons are shipped to intermediate storage facilities and then to local storage facilities (which are often banks) in the towns where they are to be issued. From there, they are taken to issuance locations where they are either prepared for mailing or disbursed directly to program participants. The issuance location can be a welfare office or a bank, post office, check-cashing business, or other business.

Retailers batch coupons and redeem them at local banks, where the retailers' accounts are credited for the value of the coupons. The banks, in turn, transmit the coupons to the regional Federal Reserve Banks, where they are physically destroyed. Deposit documents are forwarded by the banks to FNS's Computer Support Center in Minnesota, which enters the deposit information into a computerized data base and develops reports for use by FNS to monitor the system.

The many steps of the coupon flow process highlight the complexity that results from linking program benefits to food consumption through coupons. Many of these steps could be eliminated if benefits were transmitted in the form of checks. The federal costs associated with coupon issuance, most of which would be eliminated with check issuance, amount to approximately 52 cents per case month (Fraker, et al. 1992).

Monitoring Retail Outlet Compliance with Food Stamp Regulations

About 215,000 retail outlets participate in the Food Stamp Program nationwide. Food stamp regulations require that these outlets accept

Figure IV.1 COUPON FLOW

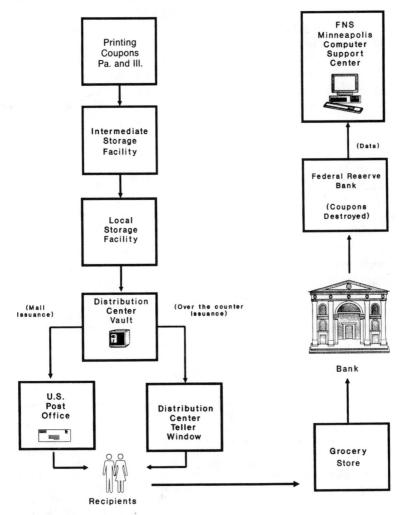

Note: Distribution center may be welfare office, bank, check cashing agency, or other organization.

coupons only in payment for food items. It is the responsibility of FNS to ensure that coupons are not exchanged for nonfood items or for cash.

Until recently, retail outlet compliance with program regulations was monitored through FNS field offices throughout the country, with field office personnel visiting retail outlets and examining the outlets' procedures for ensuring compliance on a routine basis. However, budgetary pressures have now led to phasing this out.

Currently, FNS performs statistical monitoring of the outlets, based on their characteristics and the volumes of coupons they redeem. When high redemption volume (compared to stores with similar characteristics) indicates that a store may be accepting coupons illegally, an FNS investigator poses as a client to determine whether the store is redeeming coupons illegally. Investigations are also triggered by reports by the public or local law enforcement agencies of program violations.

The amount of store fraud uncovered through this detection system is substantial. In fiscal year 1988, FNS completed 4,875 investigations. Of that number, 4,350 revealed violations of program rules and 2,825 were determined by FNS to warrant either a period of disqualification or a monetary penalty.

Considerably more retailer fraud could almost certainly be detected through stepped-up investigative efforts. The very high percentage of fraud investigations that currently uncover violations suggests that only the worst cases of wrongdoing are now being uncovered. If so, substantial additional increases in this area of program integrity could be achieved by devoting additional resources to the effort.

Notes

1. A somewhat different argument for state or local involvement in administering assistance programs hinges on allowing states or local communities to supplement federal programs with additional resources, as is done, for instance, by many states in the SSI Program. Even though the basic objectives of assistance programs may be national in scope, some states or local communities may have their own assistance-related objectives that go beyond national goals. Administration at the state or local level can help accommodate desires by states or communities to supplement assistance targets set at the federal level.

2. The numbers in the text include both reviews of active cases and reviews of negative actions.

3. U.S. Department of Agriculture, Food and Nutrition Service. "The Food Stamp Program Quality Control System: A Report to the U.S. Congress." May 1987, p. 35.

4. U.S. Department of Agriculture, Food and Nutrition Service, "The Food Stamp Program Quality Control System: A Report to the U.S. Congress," 1987.

5. In view of the tradeoffs noted earlier between ensuring program accuracy and facilitating program access, it would be particularly interesting to know whether there are significant negative correlations between error rates and participation rates.

Unfortunately, there are no reliable state level data on participation rates among eligible households.

6. U.S. Congress, House of Representatives, Committee on Ways and Means, 1992, p. 654.

7. For instance, cases with frequent changes in household circumstances—such as many of the cases with earned income—tend to be relatively expensive to administer. On the other hand, AFDC cases tend to be relatively inexpensive for the Food Stamp Program to administer, since the costs of administration are shared with the AFDC program.

8. In the context of the temporary demonstration, the simplification policies were structured so that most clients affected by the demonstration received increases in benefits. However, this feature of the demonstration raised aggregate benefit outlays and would therefore be unlikely to be included in an on-going simplification policy. If the simplification policies in the demonstration had been structured so as to keep aggregate benefits roughly constant—a much more likely form for the simplification to take if it were made permanent—there would have been substantial numbers of clients whose benefits went down.

9. The study found that the simplification policies tested had only very small effects on program participation.

10. Additional information about the demonstration and its evaluation is available in Hamilton (1987).

Chapter Five

EFFECTS OF FOOD STAMPS ON FOOD EXPENDITURES AND NUTRIENT INTAKE

Since an explicit objective of the Food Stamp Program is to "permit low-income households to obtain a more nutritious diet," it is appropriate to assess the evidence linking food stamp benefits to the food available to participant households. We begin by discussing the nutritional problems food stamps seek to address.

Instances of severe malnutrition are extremely uncommon in the United States and not obviously related to income. A report on nutrition-monitoring prepared for the Department of Health and Human Services and the Department of Agriculture concludes that the current food supply and nutrient content are "generally adequate to prevent undernutrition and deficiency-related diseases."[1] A report on national health objectives prepared by the Public Health Service comments, "In general, excesses and imbalances of some food components in the diet have replaced once-prevalent nutrient deficiencies as the principal concern."[2]

Nevertheless, there is substantial evidence of persistent hunger and shortages of food among low-income Americans. Estimates based on household food use patterns over seven days show that 61 percent of low-income American households fail to meet all the recommended dietary allowances (RDAs) examined (Table V.1).[3] The two nutrients with the lowest percentages were calcium and Vitamin B6 (59 and 62 percent, respectively).

It is important to note here that the RDAs are conservative intake standards, which should not be interpreted as minimum standards. Many people probably need less than the RDAs for most nutrients. However, failure to meet the RDAs does indicate nutritional risk.

Hunger is prevalent among America's poor according to a recent national survey of families with children who were at or below 185 percent of the poverty level but not homeless. Of the households surveyed, 94 percent said that adult household members sometimes ate less than they felt they should because there was not enough

Table V.1 LOW-INCOME HOUSEHOLDS USING FOOD THAT MET RECOMMENDED
DAILY ALLOWANCE (1979–80)

Nutrient	Percent of Households
Food Energy	73
Protein	97
Calcium	59
Iron	80
Magnesium	71
Phosphorus	93
Vitamin A	78
Thiamin	89
Riboflavin	91
Vitamin B_6	62
Vitamin B_{12}	79
Ascorbic Acid	90
All Nutrients	39

Source: U.S. Department of Agriculture, Human Nutrition Information Service, 1982.

money, and 88 percent said this was true of the children as well
(Table V.2). In addition, 95 percent said they had cut the size of or
skipped meals because there was not enough money for food, and
83 percent said they had cut the size of their children's meals. Much
lower, but nevertheless very disturbing, 33 percent said their children
sometimes had to go to bed hungry because there was not enough
money to buy food.

Nutrition-related problems may also be particularly prevalent for
low-income elderly households and for the homeless. According to
the 1979–80 Survey of Food Consumption in Low-Income Households, only 33 percent of low-income elderly households obtained
the RDA of 11 nutrients (Ponza and Wray, 1989), compared with 39
percent of all low-income households (Table V.1). A recent study of
the homeless found that 36 percent reported that they went at least
one day per week without eating any food and that on average they
eat only 1.9 meals per day (Burt and Cohen, 1988). The widespread
use of food pantries and soup kitchens is additional evidence that
many Americans cannot get enough to eat with their own resources.[4]

EFFECTS OF FOOD STAMPS ON FOOD EXPENDITURES

Statistical analyses of the effects of food stamps on food expenditures
involve: (1) comparing the food expenditures of households partici-

Table V.2 INDICATORS OF EXTENT AND DURATION OF HUNGER

	Percent Yes	Average Number of Days in Past 30 Days
Did your household ever run out of money to buy food to make a meal?	92	6.0
Did you or adult members of your household ever eat less than you felt you should because there was not enough money for food?	94	6.9
Did you or adult members of your household ever cut the size of meals or skip meals because there was not enough money for food?	95	7.1
Did your children ever eat less than you felt they should because there was not enough money for food?	88	6.7
Did you ever cut the size of your children's meals or did they ever skip meals because there was not enough money for food?	83	6.6
Did your children ever say they were hungry because there was not enough food in the house?	73	6.5
Did you ever rely on a limited number of foods to feed your children because you were running out of money to buy food for a meal?	98	10.1
Did any of your children ever go to bed hungry because there was not enough money to buy food?	33	5.5

Source: Food Research and Action Center, March, 1991, p.13.

pating in the Food Stamp Program with the expenditures of similar households not participating, and (2) comparing the food expenditures of food stamp recipients who receive different amounts of food stamps. This is the basic line of reasoning underlying such analyses:

> By determining whether households receiving food stamps have higher food expenditures than similar households not receiving food stamps, and by determining whether households receiving large amounts of food stamps have higher food expenditures than those receiving smaller amounts, we can draw inferences about whether food stamp receipt affects food expenditures. The magnitude of any observed differences between these groups gives an estimate of the size of the program effects.

An obvious potential problem with this approach is that house-holds vary by many other dimensions, in addition to food stamp receipt, which could affect food expenditures. If these are not taken into account, observed differences in food expenditures may be attrib-uted to food stamps when, in reality, they are due to one or more other factors. Various forms of statistical regression analysis have been used to control for the effects of these other variables.

Most regression studies of the effects of food stamps on food expen-ditures present their results in the form of estimates of the marginal propensity to consume (MPC) food out of food stamps. The MPC is defined as the rise in food expenditures resulting from a $1 rise in food stamps. An estimated value of, say, .28 for the MPC would imply that a dollar's worth of additional food stamps would increase food expenditures by 28 cents.

This approach to estimating the MPC can be defined at a more formal level by specifying the equation:

$$F = b_0 + b_1 S + b_2 Y + b_3 X1 + b_4 X2 + \ldots$$

where,

   F is food expenditures
   S is the value of food stamp coupons
   Y is income, including cash transfer payments

   The X variables are other variables, such as household composi-tion, region of country, and ethnic background, which may affect food expenditures

   And the b variables are parameters of the relationship which are estimated statistically.

Econometric techniques are used to estimate the parameters of this equation. Within this context, b_1, the estimated coefficient on the food stamp variable, provides an estimate of the rise in food expenditures resulting from a $1 rise in food stamps. The estimated coefficient, b_2, on the income variable provides an estimate of the rise in food expenditures resulting from a $1 rise in income.

Most of the available econometric studies of the relationship between food stamps and food expenditures have followed the approach sketched above. However, within this basic framework, a large number of methodological issues arise, which have complicated the statistical work and led to discrepant results. Among them are the following:

■ *Selection Bias.* Households that receive food stamps may differ from nonparticipating eligible households in ways that are not fully observable and therefore cannot be directly controlled for in regression analysis. This complicates interpretation of estimated regression coefficients on the food stamp variable, since these coefficients may partially reflect unobserved differences in households rather than the effects of food stamps. The econometrics literature has developed a number of techniques for dealing with this difficulty, although not totally successfully.

■ *Functional Form.* The interrelationships among variables in the food expenditure equations are quite complicated. Available economic theory about consumption behavior provides insufficient information for making clear choices regarding which of many possible functional forms to use.

■ *Controlling for Household Size and Composition.* Household size and composition may affect food expenditure relationships in many different ways, but again available theory provides no clear guidance about how to treat variation by age and gender in household composition or how to model possible economies of scale in household food consumption.

■ *Alternative Data Collection Methodologies.* Several different methods have been used by alternative surveys to obtain data on household food expenditures. Alternative data collection methodologies can lead to different estimates of expenditures, but it is not clear what types of biases are introduced by different methods.

■ *Controlling for Numbers of Meals Consumed away from Home.* Expenditures on food prepared at home vary with the proportion of meals a household buys away from home. But, the implications of various methods for adjusting for this factor are not well understood.

■ *Weighting Survey Data.* Many survey data sets related to food expenditures are based on complex sample designs and require weighting even when used for simple tabulations. The use of weighting can have important effects on the results obtained in econometric work, but there is often no strong theoretical basis on which to choose weights.

Analysts using survey data to estimate marginal propensities to consume food face complicated choices with regard to each of these issues. Other econometric decision also arise, including (1) methods for dealing with missing data, (2) data editing, (3) treatment of outlier observations, and (4) selection of statistical estimation techniques. As will be discussed below, conclusions drawn from the statistical work can be quite different, depending on the choices made on these issues.

Table V.3 shows the range of marginal propensities to consume food (MPC) out of food stamps estimated by various studies (column 4). Most studies based on data collection prior to elimination of the food stamp purchase requirement estimate marginal propensities to consume food out of food stamp benefits in the range of .20 to .50, implying that an additional dollar of food stamps increases food purchases by 20 to 50 cents. The few studies based on data collected after elimination of the purchase requirement estimate marginal propensities to consume out of food stamps in the .20 to .70 range. A recent paper (Levedahl 1991) suggests that much of the substantial variation in both sets of estimates is due to differences in functional form.

The weight of the evidence, in our judgment, indicates that the MPC is between .20 and .30. Thus, for the typical food stamp household with a benefit level of approximately $120 worth of food stamps each month, an MPC of .25 implies that food stamps increase food expenditures by approximately $30, assuming a linear expenditure model—about 11 percent of total food purchases for such households.[5] It also implies, of course, that 75 cents of every food stamp benefit dollar is not used to obtain food. This result implies less program impact on food expenditures than many advocating the use of stamps rather than cash would hope. Even so, as discussed in the next section, available evidence suggests that food stamps have more impact on food consumption than does cash assistance.

RELATIVE IMPACTS ON FOOD EXPENDITURES OF FOOD STAMPS AND CASH

Microeconomic theory suggests that the effects of food coupons on food purchases depends crucially on whether the value of coupons received exceeds the value of food the household would have bought if all purchasing power, including food assistance, had been cash. If a household's food purchases exceed the value of the direct food assistance that it receives, the household's expenditure choices are unconstrained. It can purchase the same combination of food and nonfood items, independently of whether its food assistance comes as cash or as coupons. But, if the value of food the household would buy if it received all-cash income is less than the value of its food assistance, then food coupons constrain the household in the direction of spending more on food than if the assistance came as cash.

Prior to elimination of the purchase requirement (EPR) by the Food Stamp Act of 1977 food stamp households who had income were required to purchase part of their food coupons with their own money and received coupons averaging about 40 percent of their income.[6] Under these circumstances, substantial numbers of households received more benefits in food coupons than the value of the food they would have purchased with equivalent cash.

Since EPR, however, most households receive fewer coupons than they would have received under the purchase requirement, but do not, of course, have to spend any of their own money on the stamps. It is known from survey data that most households spend more on food per month than the value of their post-EPR food stamp entitlement. Because of this, it was widely predicted that adopting EPR would mean that food stamps would have no more impact on food expenditures than direct cash transfers. According to Senator Carl Curtis of Nebraska, for example, "A food stamp user will not have to commit part of his income for food. Food stamps will not supplement his own grocery money. They will supplant it. They will merely free up his grocery money to be used in other ways."[7] The issue turns out to be less clear cut then Senator Curtis made it sound, as a comparison of columns (4) and (5) of Table V.3 indicates.

The consistently higher estimated values for the MPC out of food stamps as compared to the MPC out of money income suggest that food stamps have a larger effect on food purchases than do equivalent amounts of cash. In many of the individual studies, the differences between the two MPCs have not been statistically significant. However, the fact that this differential has been found by a number of different studies based on several different data sets—and has continued since EPR—strongly suggests that it reflects real differences in spending behavior, contrary to theoretical expectations. A number of hypotheses have been advanced.

One possible explanation is that, although *most* food stamp households purchase more food than the value of their food stamps, there remains a group of program participants for whom the constraint that food coupons be spent on food is binding because essentially all their food purchases come from coupons. Table V.4 presents 1979–80 post-EPR data for food stamp recipient households on the ratio of food stamps to total food purchases. Most food stamp households spend considerably more money on food than the value of the food stamps they receive. However, for 11 percent of the households

Table V.3 ESTIMATES OF THE MARGINAL PROPENSITY TO CONSUME FOOD AT HOME OUT OF VARIOUS INCOME SOURCES FROM SELECTED STUDIES OF LOW-INCOME HOUSEHOLDS

Study (1)	Data Used (2)	Sample Size (3)	Estimated Marginal Propensities to Consume Food from:	
			Food Stamps (4)	Money Income (5)
Studies Using Data from Before the Elimination of the Purchase Requirement				
Hymans and Shapiro (1976)	1968–1972 Michigan PSID Data	n = 3,318	.35 – .64	.14 – .17
West (1984)	1973–1974 Consumer Expenditure Diary Survey	FSP participants, n = 587;	.17	NA
		FSP eligibles, n = 2,254	.47	NA
Salathe (1980)	1973–1974 Consumer Expenditure Diary Survey	FSP participants, n = 2,254	.36	.06
Brown, Johnson, and Rizek (1982)	1977–1978 Low-Income (LI) Supplement to the Nationwide Food Consumption Survey (Weighted Data)	FSP participants, n = 911	.45	.05
Smallwood and Blaylock (1985)	1977–1978 LI Supplement to the Nationwide Food Consumption Survey (Unweighted Data)	FSP eligibles, n = 2,852	.23	.10
Chen (1983)	1977–1978 LI Supplement to the Nationwide Food Consumption Survey (Unweighted Data)	FSP participants, n = 1,809	.20	.09

			.21 – .42	.07 – .08
Devaney and Fraker (1989)	1977–1978 LI Supplement to the Nationwide Food Consumption Survey	FSP eligibles, n = 4,473	.21 – .42	.07 – .08
Studies Using Data from After the Elimination of the Purchase Requirement				
Chen (1983)	1979–1980 LI Supplement to the Nationwide Food Consumption Survey	FSP participants, n = 1,630	.23	.11
Senauer and Young (1986)	1979 Michigan PSID Data	FSP participants, n = 574	.26	.07
Fraker, Long, and Post (1990)	1985 Continuing Survey of Food Intakes of Individuals	Households eligible or FSP and WIC Program, n = 515	.29	.05
Ranney and Kushman (1987)	4-State Survey carried out in 1979–80	FSP Participants n = 310	.62	.04
Levedahl (1991)	1979–1980 Survey of Food Consumption in Low Income Households	FSP Participants n = 1,210	.69[a]	.19[a]

Source: Fraker, 1990 (excluding information on Ranney and Kushman, 1987 and Levedahl, 1991).
a. Because of non-linearities in the estimation equation, the estimated net effect of switching from food stamps to income is substantially less than the difference in the MPCs.

Table V.4 FOOD STAMP HOUSEHOLDS CLASSIFIED BY THE PERCENT OF FOOD
PURCHASES MADE WITH FOOD STAMPS

Percent of Food Purchases Made with Food Stamps	Percent of Food Stamp Households
< 50 %	53 %
51–60 %	13 %
61–70 %	7 %
71–80 %	8 %
81–90 %	5 %
91–100 %	3 %
101–110 % [a]	3 %
> 110 %	8 %

Source: Unpublished tabulations of the 1979–80 Low-Income Supplement to the 1977–78 Nationwide Food Consumption Survey.
a. Percentages greater than 100 imply that food stamp receipt was greater than food purchases during the period of measurement. This could reflect measurement error, or it could mean that food stamps were being saved until a later period. It could also reflect selling on the black market of food stamps in excess of those used to purchase food.

the value of food stamps was greater than food expenditures, suggesting that all their food purchases were made with food stamp benefits, at least over the period covered by the data collection.[8] It is likely that the MPCs for food out of food stamps are very high for many of these households, which may offset relatively low MPCs for the many households whose food purchases are greater than their food stamp receipts.

Other explanations for the differential effect on food purchases of food stamps compared to cash center around the dynamics of household budgeting and decisionmaking over the course of the monthly food stamp issuance cycle. For instance, the timing of food stamp and cash receipts over the month may be important. The standard economic model—which predicts that an unconstrained household will not alter its purchasing as a result of food stamp benefits coming in the form of coupons—assumes that households plan their food purchasing decisions over an entire month. In fact, many food stamp households have relatively low cash reserves, and their spending decisions may be significantly influenced by flows of benefit receipts. Thus, when the coupons arrive, households may purchase more food than they otherwise would; then, after the coupons run out, the household may have to purchase food from cash, adding up to more total food purchases for the month than would have been made with cash. Another possibility is that food stamps go to the person in the household who buys the food, with the natural result that they are spent on food. To the extent that cash benefits go to another household member or are more widely spread among household members, more preferences get reflected in spending patterns with cash assistance.

EFFECTS OF THE FOOD STAMP PROGRAM ON NUTRIENT AVAILABILITY AND INTAKE

The stated objective of the Food Stamp Program is not to increase *expenditures*, it is to help food stamp households "obtain a more nutritious diet." But, higher food expenditures resulting from food stamp benefits may not necessarily be associated with higher nutrient availability or nutrient intake. Additional money allocated to food purchases could be spent on buying more attractive or more convenient foods, such as better cuts of meat or more highly processed products, rather than on foods with higher nutrient content. Are higher food expenditures and the receipt of food stamps, in fact, associated with higher levels of nutrient availability and use? We consider two sets of variables directly related to nutrition: *nutrient availability*, which refers to the nutrient contents of foods used in preparing meals, and *nutrient intake*, which refers to the nutrient content of the foods actually eaten.

Food Expenditures and Nutrient Availability

To the degree that higher food expenditures tend to be associated with higher nutrient availability, this provides substantial, though indirect, evidence that the higher food expenditures resulting from food stamps are associated with higher levels of nutrition-related variables as well.

Table V.5 presents data from the 1979–80 Low Income Supplement to the Nationwide Food Consumption Survey on food expenditures and nutrient availability for low-income households. For each food expenditure category, the corresponding entry in the table shows the percentage of households for which nutrient availability was sufficient to provide household members with their Recommended Daily Allowances (RDA) for each of 11 selected nutrients.

The data show a strong positive relationship between food expendi-

Table V.5 FOOD EXPENDITURES AND NUTRIENT AVAILABILITY

Weekly Food Expenditures Per Household Member	Percentages of Households Using Food Containing RDA Amounts for 11 Selected Nutrients
Less than $8	0 %
$8–$11.99	10 %
$12–$15.99	18 %
$16–$19.99	49 %
$20 or more	75 %

Source: Based on Tables 1 and 10 of U.S. Department of Agriculture, Human Nutrition Information Service, July 1982.

tures and nutrient availability. Fewer than 20 percent of the households spending $12 to $16 per week per household member on food used food containing sufficient nutrient contents to meet household members' RDA amounts. In sharp contrast, of households spending $20 or more per person on food, 75 percent used food with sufficient nutrients to fulfill all RDA amounts for the 11 nutrients studied.

A strong positive relationship between food expenditures and nutrient availability is also reported by Basiotis et al. (1987), based on a multiple equation econometric model that controlled for a variety of household characteristics.

Statistical Analyses Relating Food Stamps Directly to Nutrient Availability and Nutrient Intake

A more direct test is to examine the relationship between food stamps and nutrient availability and intake.

A recent study by Devaney, Haines, and Moffitt (1989), using data collected after elimination of the purchase requirement, found very large effects of the Food Stamp Program on nutrient availability. Food stamps increased nutrient availability levels by 15 to 20 percent for the average food stamp household. In that study, the impact of additional food stamp benefits on the use of various nutrients was 3 to 7 times larger than the impact of additional cash income, and the differences were statistically significant. A study by Allen and Gadson (1983) found comparable though slightly smaller effects of the food stamps on nutrient availability, as did Basiotis et al. (1987).

Studies of nutrient intake show positive but somewhat smaller program impacts. Basiotis et al. (1987) estimated average program impacts on nutrient intake to be approximately 12 percent using pre-

EPR data. Rush et al. (1986) and Fraker, Long, and Post (1990) find generally positive but insignificant estimates of the effects of food stamps on intake by young children.[9]

Two studies of the nutrient intake of low-income elderly food stamp recipients also found small positive program impacts. Aiken et. al. (1985) found that the program increased nutrient intake by about 3 percent for six nutrients studied. Butler, Ohls, and Posner (1985) found the program increased nutrient intake by 5.6 percent for nine nutrients studied, with only one of the effects statistically significant. It is hazardous to generalize these two findings to the nonelderly food stamp population, however, both because the elderly average relatively low levels of food stamp benefit receipt and because they have different eating patterns.

EFFECTS OF CASH-OUT

In 1980, food stamp benefits were cashed out for households composed of SSI and elderly members in nine sites around the United States as part of the Food Stamp SSI/Elderly Cash-Out Demonstration sponsored by FNS. In 1982, the Commonwealth of Puerto Rico cashed out food stamps for its residents on the basis of federal legislation granting the Commonwealth increased discretion in how to administer the program but placing a ceiling on total program expenditures. More recently, a series of additional cash-out demonstrations were conducted in selected counties in Alabama and Washington State, and in San Diego County, California. These experiences with cash-out provide additional information about the effects on food expenditures and dietary intake of switching from coupons to cash benefits.

Both the SSI/Elderly study (Hollonbeck, Ohls, and Posner, 1985) and the Puerto Rico study (Devaney and Fraker, 1986) compared marginal propensities to consume (MPCs) food out of cash food stamp benefits with similar MPCs for comparison groups receiving food coupons. In the Puerto Rico study, the comparison group was drawn from a survey conducted prior to cash-out, while the SSI/Elderly study used a comparison group from sites which were similar to the cash-out sites but where the cash-out test had not been implemented. Impacts on nutrient intake (in the SSI/Elderly study) and nutrient availability (in the Puerto Rico study) were also examined. Neither study found significant differences between the effects of cash benefits and the effects of coupons.

Once again, the generalizability of the findings is not clear because the effects of cash-out may have been unusually small in these two settings. In the case of Puerto Rico, there was much more extensive trafficking in coupons on the black market than apparently occur in the mainland United States. The limits on generalizing from data on the elderly have already been noted.

An FNS summary of findings from the recent demonstrations in Alabama, Washington State, and San Diego County concluded that cash-out apparently reduced the food expenditures of food stamp households in three of the four demonstrations, with the sizes of the reductions ranging from 5 to 20 percent. In addition, cash-out may have had some negative effects on the availability of some nutrients; however, the findings in this area were less clear cut. Cash-out did not have significant effects on the incidence of acute food shortages among participant families (U.S., FNS, 1993; for additional details on two of the demonstrations, see Fraker et al. 1992 and Ohls et al. 1992).

These findings are broadly consistent with the results from the econometric literature discussed earlier. It appears that food stamps probably do have a greater effect on food expenditures than does cash income; however, the differences in the impacts of coupons versus cash are relatively small.

Another group of food stamp recipients whose benefits were cashed out prior to 1988 are SSI recipients in a small number of states where food stamp benefits have been added to SSI payments. No evaluations of the effects of these cash-out experiences have been undertaken, because the amount of food stamp benefits cashed out per household has been very low in these states, due to their generous SSI levels.

Notes

1. Life Sciences Research Office, 1989, p. 48.

2. U.S. Department of Health and Human Services, Public Health Service, 1991, p. 56.

3. The numbers in the table, which are based on the 1977–78 Nationwide Food Consumption Survey, are now somewhat dated but are the latest comparable data available. It is unlikely that later data would be greatly different.

4. Second Harvest, a nonprofit Chicago-based organization that provides food for distribution to the poor, provided food to more than 22,000 food pantries and 3,000 soup kitchens around the country during 1992. (Based on personal communication with R. Crane of Second Harvest, March 15, 1993.)

5. Data from Table 9 of U.S. Department of Agriculture, Human Nutrition Information Service, July 1982, show that average monthly food purchases for food prepared at home were approximately $208 per month for food stamp participants in early 1980. Adjusting for inflation since then raises this figure to approximately $270.

6. Unpublished tabulations of 1977–78 Nationwide Food Consumption Survey data.

7. U.S. Congress, Senate, Committee on Agriculture, Nutrition, and Forestry, 1985.

8. Entries in the table are based on food stamp receipts divided by food purchases. However, because of data limitations, food purchases are estimated based on the value of purchased food *used* in the previous week (multiplied by 4.3 weeks per month), while the food stamp variable is based on reported monthly value of food stamps received. Thus the ratio tabulated in the table could be influenced by unevenness in food use over time. The table entries should be viewed as only *approximations* of the long-term ratio between food stamp receipt and food purchases.

9. The two studies yield inconsistent and statistically insignificant estimates of the effects of food stamps on the intake of those nutrients by WIC-eligible women. The primary objective of Rush et al. (1986) was to estimate the effects of the WIC program on dietary intake. Fraker, Long, and Post (1990) analyzed the joint effects of WIC and food stamps on dietary intake. The samples for these studies were restricted to households eligible to receive WIC benefits.

Chapter Six

EFFECTS ON WORK INCENTIVES AND WELFARE DEPENDENCE

A major focus of welfare policy discussions during the past decade has been finding ways to reduce recipients' dependence on public assistance.

One set of questions involves the effects on labor market work of current assistance program benefits:

- Do assistance programs as currently structured significantly affect participants' work behavior?
- If so, by how much?
- What would be the work incentive effects of modest changes in existing benefit determination rules?

A second set of questions involves the effectiveness of direct efforts to increase employment among program recipients:

- Can employment of public assistance recipients be significantly increased through specific requirements that they actively search for employment?
- Can provision of employment and training services to public assistance recipients increase their employment?
- If so, are such services cost-effective?
- Are employment-related services more effective for some groups than for others?

We discuss these issues in the context of the Food Stamp Employment and Training Program. The first section provides a context for the discussion by reviewing work-related characteristics of the food stamp population.

Table VI.1 EMPLOYMENT-RELATED CHARACTERISTICS OF FOOD STAMP
RECIPIENTS

Household Characteristics	Percent
All Food Stamp Households	
One- and Two-Person Households with an Elderly Member[a]	17.6
One- or Two-Person Households with a Disabled Member[b] (Without Elderly)	5.8
AFDC Households	40.7
Other Households with Wage Income	13.6
Other Households without Wage Income	22.2
	100.0
Households Without Wage Income that Contain Potential Workers[c]	
Years of Education of Head of Household[d]	
0–11	48.9
12	41.5
More than 12	9.6
Gender of Head of Household	
Male	44.0
Female	56.0
Number of Persons in Household	
1	53.5
2	12.7
More than 2	33.9

Source: Summer 1988 Food Stamp Quality Control Sample.
a. At least one member age 60 or older.
b. At least one member receiving SSI and under age 60.
c. Households in last category of previous panel.
d. Distribution of years of education considers only those households for whom this information is available for the head of household.

EMPLOYMENT-RELATED CHARACTERISTICS OF FOOD STAMP RECIPIENTS

Most food stamp households have household members who work, are too old or disabled to work or are already subject to the work requirements of other public assistance programs (primarily the AFDC JOBS program). As shown in table VI.1, about 23 percent of food stamp households have elderly or disabled members and are small, making it unlikely that many households in this group have members who would be expected to work. Another 41 percent are AFDC households and are subject to AFDC work requirements, independently of any requirements that may be imposed by the Food

Stamp Program.[1] Another 14 percent of the households already have earnings. Thus, 75 to 80 percent of food stamp households are either unable to work or are subject to the work rules of another assistance program.

As shown in the bottom part of the table, about half of these households have heads with less than a high school education. Less than half of the heads of these households are male, and more than half are persons living alone.

TAX RATES AND WORK INCENTIVES

Much of the econometric research on the effects of assistance benefits on work incentives has been undertaken in connection with a series of social experiments conducted in the late 1960s and early 1970s. These experiments tested the effects of negative income tax programs in which randomly selected households were guaranteed a base income, and support payments were reduced by a prespecified benefit reduction tax rate as earnings increased. Several different income support levels and benefit reduction rates were tried in order to see how sensitive work effort is to changes in benefit levels and tax rates. The findings of those studies suggest that the labor supply of low-income households is not highly sensitive to small or moderate changes either in the overall size of assistance payment levels or in the marginal tax rates on earnings.

The Food Stamp Program levies a tax rate of 24 to 36 percent on a household's earnings, depending on its housing costs and other income and deductions. The findings of the negative income tax experiments summarized in Table VI.2 suggest that a 10 cent per dollar increase in the effective benefit reduction rate—from, for instance, 24 to 34 percent—would have virtually no effect on the labor supply of male wage earners in food stamp households and would reduce the labor supply of female heads of households by only about 2 percent. An increase of 20 percent in the maximum food stamp benefit levels would have an estimated effect on labor supply of only about 2 percent.

Similar conclusions were obtained in an econometric study of the labor supply of female-headed food stamp households (Fraker and Moffitt, 1988). Using data form the late 1970s, when effective tax rates in the AFDC program were considerably lower than they are

Table VI.2 ESTIMATED PARTICIPANT LABOR SUPPLY RESPONSES TO ALTERNA-
TIVE PROGRAM CHANGES

	Potential Policy Change	
	Estimated Changes in Work Effort from Increasing the Marginal Tax Rate from .24 to .34	Estimated Changes in Work Effort from Increasing the Maximum Benefit Guarantee Levels by 20 Percent
Males	0[a]	− 2 percent
Female Heads of Households	− 2 percent	− 1 percent
Wives in Husband/Wife Households	− 1 percent	− 2 percent

Note: Adapted from Table 3 of Burtless (1986). Burtless's "weighted negative income tax estimates" were used.
a. Less than half of 1 percent.

now, this study estimated that in aggregate, the Food Stamp Program reduces the labor supply of female heads of households by about 9 percent, and small to moderate changes in either the maximum benefit level amounts or the effective benefit reduction rates would change this very little.

The studies summarized so far focus on labor supply of married adults and female heads of households with children. Less analysis has been done on the labor supply of unmarried adults without children. However, a recent study of this group found that they respond considerably more to changes in marginal tax rates and benefit guarantee levels. In particular, the results obtained by Fraker and Moffitt (1989) suggest that an increase in the marginal benefit reduction rate from 24 to 34 percent could reduce labor supply by as much as 10 percent for this group and that an increase in guarantee levels of 20 percent could reduce labor supply by about 5 percent.

In assessing both the findings of the negative income tax experiments and the Fraker-Moffitt studies, it is important to note that they are based principally on data for households facing marginal tax rates in the range of .20 to .70. Thus, they are not directly applicable to the situation of households facing extremely high marginal tax rates, as is the case with many joint AFDC and food stamp households under changes made in the AFDC program in the early 1980s.[2] The inhibiting effects of transfer programs on work effort for households facing rates approaching 100 percent are almost certainly considerably greater.

WORK REQUIREMENTS AND PROGRAMS AIMED AT PROVIDING DIRECT ASSISTANCE IN HELPING PUBLIC ASSISTANCE RECIPIENTS GAIN EMPLOYMENT

Since 1971, able-bodied adult members of food stamp households who were not responsible for dependent care have been required to seek employment and accept suitable work. However, during most of the 1970s, enforcement of this requirement was, at best, uneven (U.S. General Accounting Office, 1979).

Widespread dissatisfaction in Congress with the effectiveness of the program's employment requirements led to legislation mandating two sets of demonstration projects. The first set authorized in the Food Stamp Act of 1977 and begun in 1979, involved a "workfare" approach, under which recipients were required to perform work, generally in public agencies, as a condition for remaining eligible for their benefits. Eligible food stamp work registrants in the demonstration were required to work off the value of their household's monthly coupon allotments at the federal minimum wage. If a person refused without good cause, the household lost that person's share of food stamp benefits for one month. (Subsequent refusals to comply with the program requirements could then lead to additional one-month losses of benefits.)

On balance, according to Kondratas and Nichols (1987) and the U.S. Department of Agriculture ("Final Report . . .," 1987) program effects were small. Findings include the following:

■ Turnover was so rapid (recipients averaged less than three months on the program) that many recipients left the program before all the steps involved in implementing the workfare requirement were completed, such as an initial interview and assignment to a workfare job. Of the 28,000 persons referred to one set of workfare projects, 80 percent were called in for assignment interviews, 40 percent were actually interviewed, and 20 percent worked at job sites. At some stage in the process, 12 percent of the 28,000 referred were excused for personal reasons. Only 19% were sanctioned for noncompliance.

■ Workfare neither provided the skill developments its proponents claimed, nor unduly burdened participants as critics feared. Most of those referred to workfare already had work experience. And the opportunities for skill development were limited because few remained in workfare long enough to acquire any new real skills. The workfare assignments averaged only four days of work per month.

■ The demonstration appeared to increase earnings among participants, although effects were not always statistically significant, differed among sites, and tended to be stronger for females than males.
■ Workfare reduced food stamp benefits. Benefit savings averaged $94 per participant during the first 6 months after entering the demonstration; additional savings in case-processing costs averaged $9. The benefit savings during the 6-month follow-up period amounted to a 28 percent decrease in average benefits for females and a 23 percent decrease for males. These effects apply to the 28,000 persons referred to workfare whether they actually worked at a job site or not.

In a second demonstration, food stamp work registrants were randomly assigned either to one of four work registration/job search models or to a control group not subject to any work requirements. The four models tested were:

■ An applicant Search Model, which required work registrants to complete a specified number of employer job contacts.
■ A Job Club Model, which required participation in a 2 to 4 week group session designed to improve job search skills.
■ A Group Job Search Assistance Model, which required participation in a two-day employability skills training workshop followed by eight weeks of job search with bi-weekly group meetings.
■ A Job Club/Workfare Model, which required participation in a three-week job club followed by assignment to workfare for those who failed to find a job.

All models increased earnings and reduced food stamp costs, with the job club/workfare model having the largest effect (Hausman et al., 1986). The models were also generally cost-effective, with the applicant job search and job club/workfare models having the largest benefit-cost ratios. Among other key findings were: (1) about two-thirds of the food stamp applicants at the demonstration sites were exempt from work requirements due to age, disability, participation in another program, or other factors; (2) gains in employment tended to be larger for women than for men; and (3) the average reduction in food stamp benefits for participants was about 15 percent. This 15 percent benefit reduction includes the effects of terminating benefits for clients who didn't comply with the demonstration requirements.

Further evidence on the potential effectiveness of employment and training programs is provided by the evaluation of a number of state work initiatives for AFDC recipients. In the early 1980s several states developed employment and training programs under federal legislation giving states not only authority to make workfare mandatory but also greater flexibility in developing approaches geared toward local conditions.

The employment and training components varied, but mandatory job search followed by unpaid work experience (a version of workfare) for those who had not already obtained a paid job was a common combination. Of the 13 AFDC experimental welfare-to-work programs highlighted in a recent overview of these demonstrations, eight included job search activities and seven included unpaid work experience. A few sites provided on-the-job training programs or other educational and training services (Gueron and Pauly, 1991).

While too few demonstrations have taken place to allow reliable, statistically valid generalizations to the nation as a whole, the results of the evaluations suggest a number of tentative conclusions:

- It is feasible to operate a program with mandatory employment and training components. Most states were able to provide the job search, work experience, or other services and to sanction those not in compliance.
- The workfare jobs provided real work that supervisors and most participants viewed positively, but the entry-level assignments and short duration of jobs improved skills very little.
- The employment effects were modest but usually positive for women, minimal or absent for men. The programs generally led to welfare savings, but not all of them did so.
- The benefits generally outweighed the costs when projected over a five-year period, but again this was not true of all programs.

These findings on the AFDC work initiatives are remarkably similar to those from the food stamp workfare demonstrations. For women, the programs can be operated successfully and generally produce modest employment impacts and welfare program savings. For men, who tend to enter with more employment experience, the programs seem to be less effective.

The findings to date suggest that employment and training programs may be cost-effective for some segments of the assistance population but not for others. This raises an important policy choice. It may be that employment outcomes for some segments of the population can only be improved by intensive training and counseling programs so expensive that their costs exceed the welfare savings from the additional employment. If additional studies confirm the existence of this tradeoff, society will have to decide whether the goal of improving employment for particularly hard-to-employ groups is worth the substantial net cost increases entailed.

THE CURRENT FOOD STAMP EMPLOYMENT AND TRAINING PROGRAM

In 1985 Congress passed legislation that greatly expanded the Food Stamp Program's employment and training requirements on a permanent basis. All states are now required to implement employment and training activities and to require certain groups of food stamp recipients to participate in these activities.[3]

Service Components

States are given considerable flexibility in the types of employment and training services they provide. These include:

- Job search
- Job search training
- Vocational training
- Education
- Workfare
- Work experience

Job search involves requiring recipients to make specified numbers of contacts with prospective employers over defined periods of time. At the state's discretion, these contacts can be made independently by the food stamp recipient and then reported to the Employment and Training Program, or they can be made under the direct supervision of a counselor from the program. Job search training focuses on giving participants instruction on how to look for a job and how to assess their skills and develop realistic job search objectives. Vocational training involves instruction in skills related directly to performing specific jobs. Education focuses on developing skills needed to enhance participants' employability more generally. Workfare, as noted above, requires that clients work off their food stamp benefits at a predetermined wage rate. Work experience involves placing food

FIGURE VI.1 EMPLOYMENT AND TRAINING PROGRAM SERVICES PLANNED BY
THE STATES, FY 1988

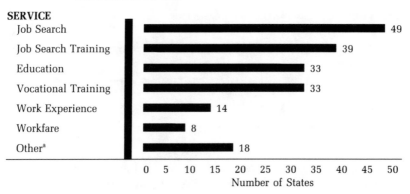

Source: Puma, et al., 1990, Figure 3.2.
a. Includes: on-the-job training, supported employment, vocational rehabilitation,
and home-based employment.

stamp recipients in temporary public sector jobs to enhance their
work experience and job skills in preparation for permanent placement.

Figure VI.1 summarizes the services states offered during fiscal
year 1988. The most common was job search, offered by essentially
all the states. Most states also offered job search training, vocational
training, and education services under their programs. Work experience and workfare were offered by relatively few.

Program Participants

Under current Food Stamp Program rules, the following recipients
are excluded from work registration programs:

■ Persons responsible for caring for a child under six years old or
for an incapacitated adult
■ Full-time students
■ Persons already working at least 30 hours per week
■ Persons subject to the work requirements of another assistance
program, such as AFDC
■ Persons who are physically or mentally disabled or in treatment
or rehabilitation programs

Figure VI.2 PARTICIPATION IN FOOD STAMP PROGRAM EMPLOYMENT AND
TRAINING PROGRAM

Estimated Food Stamp Participation During 1988 (31.8 million)	????????????????????????????????? ??????????
In E&T Target Group as Defined by Federal Law (3.3 million)	????
Remaining in Target Group after State Exemptions (2.3 million)	???
E&T Participants (1.6 million)	??

Source: Puma et al., 1990, Figure 3.7.

All other food stamp recipients between the ages of 16 and 59 years old are required to register for work and actively seek employment. These work registrants constitute the basic target group for the Food Stamp Employment and Training Program. However, subject to approval by the Secretary of Agriculture, states are also allowed to exempt from mandatory participation in the Employment and Training Program certain work registrants for whom the provision of employment and training services is not likely to be cost-effective. Such categories can include, for instance: (1) residents of areas with poor local labor market conditions; (2) residents of sparsely populated areas where the provision of employment and training services is impractical; and (3) persons still in the first benefit period.

States are required to suspend the food stamp benefits of mandatory participants who fail to cooperate with the program. In addition to serving mandatory participants, the legislation requires the program to serve "to the extent . . . practicable" other food stamp recipients who volunteer for the program. However, because of limitations on the amount of funding available for the program, states are excused from serving most of their "mandatory" participants. In particular, under current regulations, only 10 percent of mandatories are required to be served.

Approximately 31.8 million persons are estimated to have received food stamps at some point during the fiscal year ending 1988 (Figure VI.2). The great majority of them were not subject to the Food Stamp Program's work registration requirements because of the exclusion factors listed earlier: age, dependent care, work status, or participation in another employment program. As a result, only approximately 3.3 million food stamp recipients, approximately 10 percent of the total, were required to register for work. Nearly one million of these work registrants were exempted from the Food Stamp Employment and Training Program by state regulations, leaving approximately

2.3 million mandatory employment and training participants. At the time covered by these statistics, the percentage of mandatories that states were required to service was much higher, 50 percent, and program services were provided to approximately 1.6 million participants. Most of these participants are mandatories, though there are a small number of volunteers.

The majority of these Employment and Training Program participants were male, and more than 60 percent were between 22 and 40 years old (Table VI.3). More than half were single adults. About 25 percent had children. Nearly half had failed to complete high school. Slightly more than half had had some work experience over the previous year. Only 21 percent had never worked.

Impacts of the Program

A recent evaluation of the Food Stamp Employment and Training Program concluded that subjecting food stamp recipients to the program "had no discernible effect on participants' aggregate earnings, probability of finding work, amount of time worked, or average wages" (Puma, et al., 1990). Substantial numbers of E&T Program participants did find employment while in the program, but comparable numbers of a randomly selected control group also found work during the same period, yielding no net impact.

These results apply only to fiscal year 1988, the first year of operation for the E&T Program. Some program changes have been made since then, but they are minor and unlikely to have significantly increased the program's success.

One probable reason for failure is the relatively few resources devoted to the program. Despite considerable rhetoric about the government helping food stamp recipients become self-sufficient, in the year that the evaluation was conducted government spending on the program was just $135 per E&T Program participant, with referral to a job search program being the main service offered.

CONCLUSIONS

Helping public assistance recipients find jobs, thereby reducing dependence on welfare programs, has become a major public objective. Policy discussions within the context of the Food Stamp Pro-

Table VI.3 CHARACTERISTICS OF E&T PROGRAM PARTICIPANTS, FY 1988

	Percent
Demographic Characteristics	
Gender	
Male	56.3
Age	
Under 22	17.0
22–30	32.1
31–40	28.9
Over 40	21.9
Marital Status	
Currently married	22.9
Divorced, widowed, separated	29.7
Never married	47.4
Ethnicity	
White	47.6
Black	45.1
Hispanic	6.2
Other	1.1
Household Characteristics	
Average Household Size	2.24
Average Number of E&T Participants	1.24
Household Composition	
Single adults	55.7
Multiple adults, no child(ren)	19.0
Households with child(ren)	25.3
Total Income in Last 12 Months	
Less than $3,001	61.2
$3,001–$6,000	19.2
$6,001–$9,000	9.5
$9,001–$12,000	4.8
$12,001–$15,000	2.5
More than $15,000	2.8
Education	
Less than grade 12	49.5
High school graduate	30.4
Graduate equivalent diploma	7.7
Some college	10.7
College graduate	1.8
Labor Market Experience	
Worked during last 12 months	52.8
Worked, but not during the last 12 months	26.2
Never worked	21.0

Source: Puma, et al. 1990.

gram have focused on two key issues: (1) To what degree do changes in basic program benefit levels and in implicit tax rates affect work efforts? (2) Can effective programs be developed to enforce labor force participation requirements and to help recipients find employment?

Moderate changes in Food Stamp Program basic benefit levels or implicit tax rates are not likely to have substantial effects on labor supply for married persons or female heads of households, according to available evidence. Effects may be larger for unmarried adults without dependents.

A number of pilot projects have tested alternative ways of helping food stamp recipients find jobs, and a major new Food Stamp Employment and Training Program has recently been implemented. The results of the pilot programs and preliminary information from the new program suggest several conclusions:

■ There is some potential for helping food stamp recipients find employment. Such programs seem to be particularly effective in helping female recipients with relatively little previous employment experience.

■ The proportion of food stamp recipients who can potentially be helped is small. The target population of the Food Stamp Employment and Training Program, for example, is only 10 percent of food stamp recipients.

■ The funding of the current Food Stamp Employment and Training Program is too low to have a significant impact on the employment of its target population.

■ Employment and training programs can be cost-effective for some groups. This is true even from the narrow public sector perspective (Maxfield, 1990). When the increased earnings of clients are included as benefits, measured cost-effectiveness increases.

■ Employment and training programs are not cost-effective for other groups. This raises the question: is it desirable to attempt to increase employment outcomes for assistance recipients through expensive training and counseling programs, even if the net effect is to increase the public sector costs? The answer depends on the value society places on employment for its own sake.

Notes

1. Some of these households are exempted from actual participation in the AFDC JOBS programs, either because they are single parents with small children or for other reasons.

2. The current AFDC program regulations concerning the calculation of benefits are described in U.S. Congress, House of Representatives, Committee on Ways and Means (1992).

3. The discussion draws heavily on the evaluation of the project prepared by Puma et al., 1990.

Chapter Seven

THE POLITICS OF FOOD STAMPS

Our discussion so far has been couched in terms of program design tradeoffs, without much attention to the political context within which such tradeoffs are ultimately made. In this chapter we turn to the politics of food stamp policy. The tradeoff between generosity and cost is particularly important in this arena, even though it is sometimes phrased in terms of more technical issues. This chapter provides a glimpse of the behind-the-scenes give and take of legislative politics in the United States. We focus on the legislative process, because food stamp legislation tends to be very detailed, leaving relatively few details to administrative discretion as reflected in program regulations. Over the past 15 years, as we have seen, Congress has enacted legislation that contains very detailed criteria for eligibility and benefit determination and administrative procedures.

We first highlight the major features of the political environment in which food stamp policy is made. We then present a case history of the enactment of the Mickey Leland Memorial Domestic Hunger Relief Act, passed by congress in October 1990 as part of the Food, Agriculture, Conservation, and Trade Act of 1990 (P.L. 101-624). We end the chapter by drawing on this case history, together with the other material presented in this chapter, to examine five key questions:[1]

■ *What are the underlying forces that lead to food stamp legislation?* What changes external to the Congress lead legislators to propose and ultimately pass legislation about the Food Stamp Program?
■ *Who are the effective decision makers in the food stamp legislative process?* What aspects of the program and the political process determine the locus of decisionmaking? Does this process represent all the constituencies affected by food stamp legislation?
■ *Why has political support for the Food Stamp Program been consistently strong over the past 15 years?* What factors account for the ongoing, and often bipartisan, support that the program has received?

■ Does placing responsibility for the Food Stamp Program with the House and Senate Agricultural Committees best serve the interests of the poor? What are the implications for coordination with other assistance programs, the expertise of the legislators involved in setting food stamp policy, and the political strength of the program?
■ Is the legislative process underlying the Food Stamp Program efficient? What levels of time commitments are required of the key actors in enacting legislation? Are these resources used effectively? Are there effective communications among the participants in the policy formulation process?

POLITICAL ENVIRONMENT OF THE FOOD STAMP PROGRAM

Three features of the political environment of food stamps are crucial to understanding the food stamp policy process:[2]

■ The Food Stamp Program's ties with agriculture
■ The emotional strength of the hunger issue
■ Public opinion about welfare and in-kind assistance

The Food Stamp Program's Ties with Agriculture

As discussed in Chapter I, the original impetus behind the Food Stamp Program was to increase consumption of agricultural commodities. Although attention has turned increasingly to the income maintenance goal of the Food Stamp Program, its historical links with agriculture continue to shape food stamp policy.

The link between the Food Stamp Program and agriculture have traditionally made the program more attractive than other forms of income maintenance to Republican legislators with rural constituencies. Congressman Bill Emerson of Missouri, Senator Robert Dole of Kansas, and former Senator Rudy Boschwitz of Minnesota—all conservative Republicans from rural states—have been strong supporters of the program. On the Democratic side, perhaps the most influential advocate for the Food Stamp Program over the past decade has been Leon Panetta, former head of the House Budget Committee, who represented a relatively rural California district.

Supporting food stamps has also helped urban-based legislators wishing to broaden their visibility. For example, in the late 1950s, when John F. Kennedy first focused his attention on the idea of using food stamps to assist the poor, his interest at least partially reflected his desire to appeal to agricultural interests in preparation for the 1960 presidential election. The Food Stamp Program allowed him to do this, while also addressing poverty in urban areas, his traditional constituency (Maney, 1989, pp. 23–25).

Emotional Strength of the Hunger Issue

Americans feel strongly that having enough food is a basic right, and that ensuring access to enough food is a legitimate and important area of public policy. The emotional appeal of the hunger issue in this country has generated widespread support for the Food Stamp Program.

At several key points in the program's history, its advocates have been able to marshall strong public support for expanding the program by pointing to American households in poverty without enough to eat. A well-publicized field trip to Mississippi by Senators Robert Kennedy and Joseph Clark in 1967 helped program advocates marshall support for persuading USDA to reduce the purchase price of food stamps later that year. Two key factors that generated support for a 1970–1971 program expansion were (1) "Hunger in America," a 1968 CBS television documentary showing the inadequate food available to many impoverished Southern households, and (2) widely publicized hearings on hunger, conducted by Senator George McGovern, the head of the Senate Select Committee on Nutrition and Human Needs. Wide media coverage of the plight of homeless persons helped spur strong bipartisan support for the Hunger Prevention Act of 1988, which expanded program benefit levels and introduced several other changes to increase access to food stamps.

Public Opinion about Welfare and In-Kind Assistance

Although the U.S. public appears to show widespread support for helping the poor, it is uneasy about cash grant programs. In a public opinion survey conducted in 1992, 64 percent of respondents indicated that there was too little "assistance for the poor," while only 13 percent indicated that there was too much assistance. But when a comparable sample of respondents was asked about spending on "welfare," only 23 percent thought that there was too little spending on welfare, while 44 percent thought that there was too much (Toner, 1992). The Food Stamp Program provides a way to assist the poor without giving them cash, making it an attractive form of assistance to many voters.

THE MICKEY LELAND MEMORIAL DOMESTIC HUNGER RELIEF ACT

Passage of the most recent Food Stamp Program reauthorization legislation, the Mickey Leland Memorial Domestic Hunger Relief Act of 1990, shows how an ambitious initiative for significant program expansion was sidetracked; it also highlights not only the complexities but also the politics of behind-the-scenes discussions on detailed technical issues.

In July 1989, House Budget Committee Chairman Leon Panetta called the leaders of the two main food stamp client advocacy groups—the Food Research and Action Center and the Center on Budget and Policy Priorities—to his office to tell them that he was anxious to pass legislation in 1990 that would address the hunger problem and that he thought sufficient support could be mustered to enact a modest increase in government outlays in this area. Panetta asked the advocacy group leaders for their views as to how these funds could be most effectively spent.

As the discussion proceeded, the three participants in the meeting quickly focused on making changes in the Food Stamp Program as being a particularly attractive way of accomplishing Panetta's objectives. The Food Stamp Program was scheduled for reauthorization in 1990. All food stamp legislative decisionmakers viewed this as providing a context in which substantive program changes could be made. But until their meeting with Panetta, the client advocacy groups had been pessimistic that significant new resources could be added in the 1990 legislation. The Hunger Prevention Act of 1988 had recently increased program benefit outlays, and, in light of pressure to reduce the size of the federal deficit, the advocacy groups had felt that Congress would be unwilling to liberalize the program further in 1990.

Panetta's interest in strengthening the program appeared to change this assessment. As chairman of the House Budget Committee, he was in an excellent position to identify budgetary resources that could be added to the Food Stamp Program during the 1990 session. His expressed interest in expanding the program during the 1990 reauthorization significantly raised the perceived chances of doing so.

After the July meeting, the two advocacy group leaders, together with a member of Panetta's staff, began to examine alternatives for allocating additional resources to the program in ways that would most benefit the poor. At the same time, members of the Bush Administration were developing their own food stamp legislative agenda for 1990, and a few House and Senate members and their staffs were beginning to discuss what should be included in the 1990 reauthorizing legislation. Several other private organizations were also preparing for the 1990 reauthorization process.

Staking Out Positions

HOUSE OF REPRESENTATIVES

House legislation that affects the Food Stamp Program is referred to the House Agriculture Committee and, through that committee, to the Subcommittee on Domestic Marketing, Consumer Relations, and Nutrition. In 1990, that subcommittee was chaired by Representative Charles Hatcher, a Democrat representing a largely rural constituency in Georgia. Hatcher had just taken over the chair of the subcommittee from Panetta in 1989, and had only relatively limited experience with food stamp issues. The ranking minority member of the subcommittee was Representative Bill Emerson of Missouri. Emerson, a strong supporter of the program, had occupied that position since 1983 and had extensive experience with Food Stamp Program legislation. Another key representative for food stamp legislation was the Chairman of the House Agriculture Committee, Kika de la Garza, who was widely viewed as a supporter of the Food Stamp Program.

In order to maximize the chances of passing legislation that would expand the resources allocated to the Food Stamp Program, the support of both Hatcher and Emerson was critical. Support from Emerson was particularly important, to give the proposal bipartisan support and to gain votes from Republican members of the House, who look to Emerson for leadership in the area of nutrition. Panetta approached both Emerson and Hatcher about the idea of a joint bill that would increase program benefit outlays. Both Hatcher and Emerson responded positively.

Three House Agriculture Committee staff members are assigned to the Subcommittee on Domestic Marketing, Consumer Relations, and Nutrition. Two of these staff members—one working for the majority members, and one working for the minority members of the subcommittee—were directly involved in developing food stamp legislation in 1990. During the months following Panetta's initial discussions with Hatcher and Emerson, a member of Panetta's staff worked closely with these two subcommittee staffers to develop a legislative package that would be acceptable to all members of the subcommittee. In addition, as discussed more fully later, these individuals held extensive discussions with other important actors in food stamp policy, both within and outside of the government, to identify the issues that would be debated in the upcoming reauthorization legislation.

During this preliminary stage, both Hatcher and Emerson made it clear that they believed that the upcoming legislation should allocate significant resources to commodities distribution programs *in addition to* expanding the Food Stamp Program. They were also very interested in policies to simplify the Food Stamp Program and to coordinate it more effectively with other assistance programs. The legislation which was ultimately introduced in the House reflected these structural concerns. As part of developing a legislative package for reauthorizing the Food Stamp Program, the House subcommittee also held nine public hearings, some in Washington and some in other cities across the country, about the current program and its potential improvements.

THE SENATE

Food stamp legislation in the Senate is under the purview of the Senate Committee on Agriculture, Nutrition, and Forestry. That committee's subcommittee, the Subcommittee on Nutrition and Investigation, has responsibility for food stamp legislation. However, like most subcommittees of the Senate's agriculture committee, this subcommittee does not have a separate staff. Thus, much of the food stamp legislative process in the Senate takes place at the full committee level, rather than in the subcommittee as in the House.

Key Senators involved in developing food stamp legislation were Patrick Leahy (Dem., VT), Chairman of the Senate Agriculture Committee; Richard Lugar (Rep., IN), ranking minority member on the full committee; Robert Dole (Rep., KS), the Senate Minority Leader and a long time supporter of the Food Stamp Program; and Tom Harkin (Dem., IA) and Rudy Boschwitz (Rep., MN), chair and ranking minority member of the Subcommittee on Nutrition and Investigations.

As on the House side, these legislators and their staffs began meeting with one another and with outside groups in late 1989 and early 1990, to identify the important food stamp issues that would be raised in the 1990 legislative process (as discussed below) and to develop their positions on these issues.

CONGRESSIONAL BUDGET OFFICE AND CONGRESSIONAL RESEARCH SERVICE

The Congressional Budget Office (CBO) and the Congressional Research Service (CRS), two organizations that provide staff support for both the House and Senate, were also involved in the planning stage for the upcoming reauthorization process. The CBO has responsibility for estimating the impacts of proposed legislation on federal costs. As is done in other policy areas, in preparation for the upcoming legislative session, the CBO staff member with direct responsibility for producing Food Stamp Program cost estimates developed a "no change" cost projection. This projection estimated the dollar cost of the program in the coming years if no legislative changes were made.

The Congressional Research Service (CRS) provides assistance to members of Congress and their staffs in examining how current programs are functioning and in assessing the potential impacts of program changes. As with the CBO, CRS has a single staff person who performs most of the organization's work on food stamp policy. He has been involved heavily in the food stamp policy process for more than a decade, serving as CRS's "institutional memory" in food stamp matters, in addition to undertaking new research as requested by members. As Congress began preparing for the 1990 legislation, congressional staffers frequently came to him for information and advice as to the likely effects of ideas that had been suggested by various constituencies in the political process.

BUSH ADMINISTRATION

As it does in most years, the U.S. Department of Agriculture (USDA) prepared for the 1990 legislative session by following a sequence of steps tied closely to the federal budgetary process. In spring 1989, senior career civil servants in the USDA, Food and Nutrition Service (FNS), Office of Analysis and Evaluation, prepared a set of briefing materials that outlined major Food Stamp Program policy alternatives and issues for consideration during the upcoming Food Stamp Program reauthorization.

These materials were reviewed by senior program operations staff within FNS and by a number of political appointees, including the Administrator of FNS and the Assistant Secretary of Agriculture for Food and Consumer Services. Potential program changes with budgetary implications were considered in the context of preliminary budgetary guidelines provided to USDA by the U.S. Office of Management and Budget (OMB).

On the basis of this work, tentative policy proposals were developed over the summer and fall of 1989 and incorporated into USDA's budget recommendations to OMB. OMB then made decisions about the recommended policy positions and transmitted them back to USDA through a "pass back" that described the Administration's decisions.

The final food stamp proposals of the Administration were then summarized in a document known as the "Green Book," because of its neon green cover, released in early February 1990. Legislative language to implement the Administration's proposals was drafted and released in early March of the same year.

The Green Book proposed only relatively modest changes in the Food Stamp Program. These changes focused principally on administrative issues, rather than altering benefit amounts. Several of these provisions were included in the legislation introduced by Richard Lugar in the Senate, described below.

ADVOCACY GROUPS

The two advocacy group leaders with whom Congressman Panetta initially discussed plans for increasing Food Stamp Program benefit levels as part of the 1990 reauthorization legislation were the Executive Directors of the Food Research and Action Center (FRAC) and the Center on Budget and Policy Priorities (CBPP). FRAC is a national organization headquartered in Washington, D.C.; it represents the interests of low-income households in policy areas related to nutrition, including the Food Stamp Program, the National School Lunch Program, and the Special Supplemental Food Program for Women, Infants, and Children (WIC). FRAC has an annual budget of approximately $1.4 million and is financed primarily by grants from private foundations and corporations. The organization maintains close ties with state and local advocacy groups, and provides back-up legal services to those local groups. FRAC's Executive Director, Robert

Fersh, worked as a congressional staff person for Leon Panetta prior to joining FRAC and during that period developed a close working relationship with Panetta.

The Center on Budget and Policy Priorities, which is financed primarily by philanthropic foundations and also has a budget of approximately $1.4 million, advances liberal positions on a broad spectrum of policy issues. Unlike FRAC, the Center does not have an extensive grass roots constituency. Rather, it focuses on conducting detailed research studies on topics related to its liberal agenda. Much of its influence derives from its reputation for the accuracy and integrity of the research it produces. The Center takes a special interest in the Food Stamp Program, reflecting the fact that its Executive Director, Robert Greenstein, served as the Administrator of FNS during the Carter Administration and has extensive technical expertise on all aspects of the program. All members of the Washington food stamp policy community, regardless of political orientation, regard Greenstein as perhaps the most knowledgeable person in Washington on technical food stamp matters. His reliable advice on technical issues affords him close access to both liberals and conservatives and gives him extensive opportunities to influence the food stamp legislative process.

After the initial meeting with Rep. Panetta, FRAC and CBPP began discussions with Panetta's staff both about substantive program changes and about the political and legislative strategies necessary for marshalling political support. During this process, FRAC and CBPP staff members also met frequently with the other main actors in the food stamp policy process, including members of Congress and their staffs, representatives of the Bush Administration, and other private groups. FRAC, in particular, was closely involved in the day-to-day decisions about the substantive and political strategies associated with the emerging legislation.

In addition, during the latter part of 1989, FRAC and the CBPP began to stimulate political support for Food Stamp Program expansion among other advocacy groups. In November, the two organizations held a joint briefing for other interest groups, in which they summarized the key issues for the upcoming reauthorization legislation. FRAC obtained the formal support of more than 100 other organizations, including other client advocacy groups, church groups, and charitable organizations, for a statement of principles that argued for the importance of expanding the program. FRAC then printed a brochure listing these organizations as supporters of expansion and other program changes favored by the advocacy groups.

The outcome of this preliminary work by FRAC and CBPP was a series of informal recommendations to members of Congress and their staffs about the changes that would best expand program and how these changes could be packaged to maximize their political viability. Many of these recommendations were reflected in the bipartisan Food Stamp Program bill introduced in the House of Representatives in February 1990.

OTHER INTEREST GROUPS

Three other major groups were involved in developing the 1990 Food Stamp Program legislation.

1. *American Public Welfare Association.* The American Public Welfare Association (APWA), an organization of state and local public welfare agencies and their staffs. APWA was particularly interested in playing an active role in the 1990 food stamp legislative process because its involvement with the 1988 food stamp legislative process had been limited, and some of its members were unhappy with provisions in the Hunger Prevention Act that resulted.

In summer 1989, APWA convened a Food Stamp Reauthorization Task Force, consisting primarily of the employees of state welfare departments. This group met several times during fall 1989 and issued a set of legislative recommendations in January 1990. Key APWA objectives in the 1990 legislative process called for raising client benefits; simplifying program administration; establishing longer implementation times for legislative changes; and eliminating the states' financial penalties accrued during the mid-1980s under a quality control system that had later been substantially changed (see Chapter IV).

At the same time that APWA's formal legislative recommendations were being drafted, APWA staff began meeting with congressional, Administration, and advocacy group staff to discuss APWA's views on what should be included in the upcoming legislation. These initial meetings established lines of communication for advancing APWA's positions later in the legislative process.

2. *Food Marketing Institute.* The Food Marketing Institute (FMI) is a trade association of grocery retailers and wholesalers. It disseminates information on food retailing, organizes conventions and other meetings of food retailers, and conducts research on food retailing. In addition, FMI, which is headquartered in Washington, D.C., is actively involved with political issues that affect its members.

When food stamp legislation is being considered, FMI takes an active role in aspects that could affect food retailers. Two issues particularly important to FMI during the 1990 legislative session included (1) the potential use of electronic benefit transfer systems (EBT), under which food stamp benefit amounts are entered into client accounts on central computers and then debited by the retail stores when program participants make food purchases;[3] and (2) an Administration proposal to increase reporting requirements by retailers and to charge retailers fees for periodic reauthorizations to participate in the program.

Prior to introduction of the formal food stamp legislation in February 1990, FMI had targeted these potential aspects of the food stamp legislation as important, and had assigned a senior staff member to lead FMI's involvement in this area. The preliminary work undertaken by FMI was similar to that undertaken by most of the other special interest organizations involved in the Leland legislation. The FMI staff person assigned to the legislation met individually with members of Congress, congressional staff members, and representatives of other interest groups to explain FMI's positions on the relevant issues and to ascertain what was important to the other actors in the process.

3. Electronic Data Systems. The Electronic Data Systems (EDS) Corporation, a subsidiary of the General Motors Corporation, was to play a significant role in the 1990 legislative process. EDS is a major supplier of computer systems software and data processing services to state and local governments, and has been interested for many years in promoting increased automation in operating the Food Stamp Program at the state and local levels.

EDS was represented in the legislative process by Marshall Matz, who, during the 1970s, had been a committee staff member for the Senate Select Committee on Nutrition and Human Needs. Matz, who has been credited with playing a key role in passing food stamp legislation during that period, continues to have close connections to people involved in the food stamp policy setting process (Berry, 1984, p. 50). For example, he is close personal friends with key figures on the Hill, including Emerson, and, during 1990, he was Chairman of the Board of Directors of FRAC, one of the advocacy groups described earlier.

In preparation for the 1990 legislation, EDS invited several members of Congress and their staffs to a briefing about the potential cost savings and error reductions that EDS believed could be achieved through increased use of computer technology. The briefing included a demonstration of an advanced case management system developed by EDS. Matz also discussed the food stamp automation issues with several key participants in the legislative process.

The Formal Legislative Process

The process leading to the Leland Act as finally enacted can be viewed at two levels. The first is the formal legislative process through which legislation is introduced, committee hearings are held, amendments are made, committee reports are submitted, and legislation is ultimately enacted or rejected by Congress. This formal process becomes the public record for the legislation. This section describes the formal legislative process that led up to enactment of the Leland Act.

The second level entails informal discussions among key participants in the legislative process, leading to various compromises and agreements about what will be included in the legislation. This informal process—much less in the public view but crucial to a full understanding of how food stamp legislation is enacted—is discussed in the next section.

HOUSE LEGISLATION

Only one significant piece of food stamp legislation was introduced in the House in 1990, HR 4110. This legislation was submitted by Panetta, Hatcher, Emerson, de la Garza, and several other members of congress, including all the members of the Subcommittee on Domestic Marketing, Consumer Relations, and Nutrition. Its provisions were intended mainly to expand the program and were estimated to cost more than $1 billion per year when fully implemented. They included:

- Increasing program benefits for most participants by increasing the percentage of the Thrifty Food Plan amounts used to calculate program benefits
- Removing the ceiling on the housing expense deduction
- Increasing commodity distribution under the Temporary Emergency Food Assistance Program
- Creating a commission to study possible consolidation of procedures used in the AFDC and Food Stamp Programs
- Forgiving the fiscal liabilities of states to the federal government that had accrued in the mid-1980s as penalties for case errors under a system then in effect for sanctioning states with high error rates

■ Increasing financial incentives for implementing automated processing systems, and requiring that the Secretary of Agriculture establish standards for using electronic data processing systems to support the client certification process

■ Requiring that stores allowed by FNS to use electronic benefit transfer equipment at store checkout lanes provide EBT in all lanes[4]

These provisions were the result of several important factors. First, the bill as introduced reflected Panetta's interest in increasing benefit levels under the program, together with his assessment of both the amount of funding that could be found in the federal budget process and the changes that would receive broad support in Congress. Second, the bill was influenced heavily by input from client advocacy groups about how available resources should be spent to ensure that food stamp participants would be helped as much as possible by the program, within the context of the available resources. Third, the bill reflected the strong interest of Emerson and Hatcher in using direct commodity distribution as part of America's overall program for providing nutrition assistance to low-income households.

The bill was named after Representative Mickey Leland from Texas, who had died tragically in an airplane crash the previous year. Leland had been a strong advocate of the Food Stamp Program and other policies to reduce hunger, both in the United States and around the world, and he was highly regarded among his congressional colleagues. Several proponents of program expansion in the 1990 reauthorizing legislation felt strongly about using the legislation as a memorial to him.

The next formal House action after the Leland Act was introduced was a subcommittee "markup" session on March 21, 1990. During this meeting, the subcommittee made only minor modifications in the proposed legislation, approved the bill, and reported it back to the full House Agriculture Committee. Subcommittee approval was never in doubt, since Hatcher and Emerson had obtained the support of the subcommittee members very early in the legislative process. The high degree of consensus within the subcommittee also reflected the fact that the House was expected to pass a Budget Resolution which included funding for the program expansions envisioned in the Leland legislation. (A House budget resolution which included this funding was subsequently passed later in the spring.)

The legislation was next considered by the full House Agriculture Committee. At this point, it was combined with the rest of the 1990 farm bill, as had been intended by all participants in the process.

The Mickey Leland name was retained as applying to Title XVII of the farm bill, the section of the bill dealing with the food stamp and other domestic nutrition programs. The committee reported the entire farm bill back to the full House on July 3, again with only minor changes.

As the Leland bill came under consideration, first by the Agriculture Committee and then by the full House, the Administration lobbied against provisions that would increase federal costs, sending Betty Jo Nelsen, the FNS Administrator, and Catherine Bertini, the Assistant Secretary of Agriculture for Food and Consumer Services, to meet with key members of Congress on the issue. In general, the Administration's strategy was not to argue strongly against the merits of individual provisions of the bill, but rather to argue that food stamp spending had risen very rapidly in previous years, and that 1990 was not a good time to allocate yet more resources to the program.

While the Administration did not generally lobby against individual components of the bill, it did compile a priority list of what it regarded as particularly troublesome provisions. The order of these priorities reflected the Administration's substantive assessment of the advantages and disadvantages of the individual components of the bill, as well as strategic factors. An example of the latter was the priority ranking of the provision to remove the ceiling on the shelter deduction. The removal of the shelter deduction cap was one of the most expensive components of the proposed Leland legislation and one that the Administration was very eager to eliminate. However, the Administration did not give it top priority for elimination because it knew that Robert Greenstein strongly supported it and could mobilize substantial opposition to its removal, making elimination of shelter cap politically impossible at this stage of the legislative process. Thus, its priority list focused on other, "more vulnerable" provisions of the bill.

During the debate on the full farm bill on August 1, Congressman Bill Frenzel (Rep., MN), acting for the administration, introduced a series of amendments that would have removed from the legislation those Food Stamp Program revisions that required additional funding. These amendments were considered to be the most significant threat to the Leland Act during the House deliberations.

The importance of Panetta's gaining the strong involvement and support of Emerson for the Leland legislation became particularly evident at this point. Emerson sent several "Dear Colleague" letters to urge members of Congress to oppose the Frenzel Amendments, which probably influenced many of the substantial numbers of Republican members who opposed the Administration's amendments.

The Frenzel Amendments were defeated by a vote of 336 to 83. Long-time supporters of the Food Stamp Program regard this vote as perhaps the strongest endorsement of the program ever made by Congress. After the defeat of the Frenzel Amendments, the Leland Act was passed by the House, as part of the overall farm bill, by a vote of 318 to 102.

SENATE LEGISLATION

Three major pieces of food stamp legislation were introduced in the Senate during the late winter and early spring of 1990. On March 9, Senator Richard Lugar (Rep., IN), the ranking Republican member of the Senate Agriculture Committee, introduced an overall farm bill which, for the most part, reflected the Administration's positions. In introducing the bill, Senator Lugar said that he did not necessarily agree with all aspects of the bill, but that he was introducing it in order to put the Administration's position on the table for discussion.

The Lugar bill included provisions to (1) require that food stamp recipients participate in the Child Support Enforcement Program, when appropriate, as a condition for receiving food stamps; (2) authorize the use of EBT; and (3) increase retailer reporting requirements associated with being approved to accept food stamps. Reflecting the Administration's desire to contain program costs, the Lugar bill did not increase food stamp benefit levels or alter the ceiling on the shelter deduction, two of the key provisions being considered in the House.

Two weeks after the Lugar bill was introduced, Senators Jim Sasser (Dem., TN) and Pete Domenici (Rep., NM) introduced a second piece of proposed Senate food stamp legislation, the Hunger Prevention Act of 1990. Sasser was chairman and Domenici ranking Republican on the Senate Budget Committee. In introducing the bill, Sasser and Domenici were joined by other senators involved in food stamp legislation, including Patrick Leahy (Dem., VT), Tom Harkin (Dem., IA), and Rudy Boschwitz (Rep., MN). Leahy was the Chairman of the Senate Agriculture Committee; Harkin and Boschwitz were the chairman and ranking minority member of the Subcommittee on Nutrition and Investigations. The Sasser/Domenici bill was similar to the House bill, but proposed fewer minor changes to the program. From a technical point of view, this Sasser/Domenici bill was to be largely superseded by a similar bill developed within the Agriculture Committee under the leadership of Sen. Leahy and introduced a month later. However, the commitment to strengthening the Food Stamp Program reflected in Sasser's and Domenici's bill was extremely important, given their positions as the ranking members of the Budget Committee. Sasser and Domenici had decided to sponsor the bill after attending a Budget Committee hearing in which both program advocates and program participants argued persuasively that the program was not fully meeting the nutritional needs of many of the people it was designed to help.

The last of the three major pieces of food stamp legislation introduced in the Senate in 1990 was the Leahy bill. Its proposed title was the same as the Leland Bill in the House, and it contained similar provisions, with the single major exception that increasing the use of automated case processing systems was left out.

These three Senate bills were referred to the Senate Agriculture Committee for consideration. At this point, in late April, 1990, the key actors anticipated that the committee would recommend legislation that would increase spending on the Food Stamp Program in ways that roughly paralleled the legislation being crafted in the House.[5]

The next formal step in the legislative process on the Senate side should have been a mark-up session, either by the full Agriculture Committee or by its subcommittee. However, before a markup session could be scheduled, the Senate, on June 14, passed a fiscal year 1991 Budget Resolution, which included no money for expanding the Food Stamp Program. This resolution, combined with strong pressure from agriculture interests within the Senate Agriculture Committee not to divert authorized funds from any other parts of the farm bill, persuaded the Democratic leadership of the Agriculture Committee not to include any Food Stamp Program reauthorization in the farm bill they reported out of committee. Instead, they decided to wait until the House/Senate Conference Committee reported on the farm bill to add the Food Stamp Program's reauthorization.

Their rationale for this strategy was that passage of a bill to reauthorize the program but not to expand it could later be interpreted by the House/Senate Conference Committee as indicating the Senate's unwillingness to authorize changes that would require additional funds. In fact, virtually all the key actors still believed that the Senate *was* willing to authorize the addition of funds if budgetary resources were found, and also that budget resources *would* be found, given the presumed support of Sasser, Domenici, and Panetta. In particular, given the complex budget-related negotiations which were expected to occur over the summer, both within the Congress and between the Congress and the Administration, it was believed that an opportunity would be identified to reverse the decision in the June 14 Senate budget Resolution against allocating additional resources to the Food Stamp Program. Thus, the farm bill was passed by the Senate on July 27 without a nutrition program title.

THE CONFERENCE COMMITTEE

While these events were taking place during the spring and summer of 1990, significant changes were taking place in the overall fiscal and political environment. In particular, the federal budget deficit was growing significantly more than expected. For instance, between January and July 1990, the Administration estimate of the FY 1990 budget deficit rose from $122 billion to $218 billion, an increase of 79 percent. Even the Congressional Budget Office, which had had a better recent deficit prediction record than the Administration, had raised its estimate of the FY 1990 deficit by 41 percent. These revised estimates shrank the estimated fiscal resources available for expanding federal programs.

In light of this tightening budget situation, by the time that the Farm Bill Conference Committee began meeting on September 19, 1990, the optimism of the spring about being able to pass an expansionary food stamp bill had faded substantially. Nevertheless, even at this point, many participants in the process believed that there was at least some possibility that this could still be achieved. However, the protracted negotiations over the FY 1991 budget derailed these hopes. Despite efforts by Panetta to retain funding for the Leland provision, the final outcome of these talks, reached in October, was a budget that did not include additional funds for the Food Stamp Program. Thus, it was necessary to delete the benefit expansion provisions of the Leland Act as passed in the House.

Numerous technical decisions about proposed program changes remained to be resolved, before the final food stamp reauthorization legislation could be passed. These included whether and under what circumstances to allow EBT, how to set and enforce standards for case processing automation, and how to increase coordination between AFDC and food stamps.

Most of the final decisions on these issues were made with no legislators present, during two marathon meetings organized and attended by the relevant congressional staffers. These meetings, the second of which extended into the early morning hours, had no designated chair, and participants describe them as very unstructured. In addition to congressional staff, senior members of the Administration, including the FNS Administrator and the USDA Assistant Secretary for Food and Consumer Services, were present. No representatives of any of the advocacy groups or other private organizations were invited or present. The basic mode of decision-making appears to have been to talk through each issue until everybody was willing to agree. Such agreements were subject to later renegotiation, based on subsequent decisions of the meeting.

The absence of any legislators at this meeting reflects several factors. First, by this point in the process, the relevant issues had been sufficiently circumscribed through the discussions and legislative actions which had taken place through the spring and summer that there was only limited scope for significant change. Second, in general, the legislators were confident that their aides fully understood their positions, through the interactions which had occurred up to that point. Finally, if any decision had been made which created serious problems for one of the key legislators, that decision could still have been reexamined during the formal Conference Committee proceedings.

The outcome of the meetings was a set of decisions that were then translated into the legislative provisions of the Conference Committee report. No substantive changes were made by the Conference Committee itself.

The Conference Committee completed its work on the farm bill on October 22. The nutrition title of the bill, which continued to be named after Mickey Leland, reauthorized the Food Stamp Program for another five years, and introduced several relatively small program changes. The farm bill, including the nutrition title, was subsequently passed in both houses by substantial margins.

Why were the sponsors of the original Leland Act provisions so wrong in believing that funding would be found for Food Stamp Program expansion? Similarly, why were the advocacy groups, who strongly supported the expansionary provisions of the bill and who often have considerable political power in food stamp issues, not able to mobilize sufficient support to force passage of expanded benefits?

One factor in answering these questions is the use of the "Budget Summit" mechanism to enforce fiscal constraint in 1990. This significantly altered the rules of the game. While Panetta and Sasser were, of course, important participants in these talks, they had considerably less room to maneuver in these talks than in their own committee deliberations.

The shift of the decision making venue to the budget summit talks also limited the influence of the advocacy groups in the final decision making process. Greenstein and the staff of FRAC had very limited access to the budget summit negotiations. Also, as noted earlier, much of their ability to influence food stamp policy comes from the congressional respect accorded to their technical expertise. At the budget talks, framing of the food stamp expansion issue directly in terms of dollars took away the force of the technical expertise weapon.

Behind the Scenes: The Give and Take of Legislative Politics

None of the decisions reflected in the final food stamp legislation were, in fact, made during formal legislative sessions, either by the committees or by the full House or Senate. Decisions were *ratified* during these formal sessions but *determined* during informal discussions.

Beginning in mid-1989 and continuing through final enactment of the Leland Act, members of Congress, congressional staff, officials of the Bush Administration, representatives of the client advocacy groups, and members of other private organizations all met frequently.

These meetings were recognized by all participants as serving several purposes. First, frequent informal conversations made it possible for each participant to assess the chances of various options and initiatives by finding out the reactions of other participants. In addition, informal discussions provided a context for attempting to change the opinions of other participants about various issues of particular concern. Meetings were also used to develop compromise positions and to strike deals in which one person's support for one issue was traded off against another person's support for a different issue.

Second, these meetings allowed various actors to comment informally on draft legislative language or proposals for new draft language. Many of the Leland Act provisions were written and rewritten several times during the legislative process, both to reflect changes in positions by various participants and to deal with technical issues as they arose during the review of draft language.

This informal give and take during the legislative process consumed considerable amounts of time. During the first half of 1990, for example, two congressional staff members worked essentially full time on the Leland Bill, with much of their time devoted to these informal discussions. At least three other people, two in the Administration and one staff member of the APWA, devoted at least half of their work time to the process. Several others, including congressional staff members, Administration officials, and representatives of various interest groups, spent up to one-third of their time on matters related to the bill during all or part of the legislative process.

The informal parts of the legislative process consist largely of discussions that do not make it to the public record. To convey a sense of how the informal discussions and negotiations were carried out, we trace the evolution of four provisions of the 1990 legislation:

- Eliminating the ceiling on the shelter deduction (the only benefit-expanding provision we examine)
- Allowing states to use EBT to issue program benefits
- Setting standards for the states to use automated data systems to maintain and process program information
- Coordinating the Food Stamp Program with the Child Support Enforcement Program

ELIMINATING THE CEILING ON THE SHELTER DEDUCTION

As soon as it became apparent that budgetary resources might be available for expanding the Food Stamp Program, advocacy groups and interested members of Congress argued for eliminating the shelter deduction ceiling. This change was an attractive way to substantially increase benefits,[6] particularly for households with very high housing costs. It was also politically attractive, because it could be construed as a technical change in the program, rather than as a wholesale program expansion. To be sure, it was fully understood by the legislators involved that the change would lead to increased program costs. Nevertheless, the expansion of the housing deduction could be characterized as simply extending to other parts of the caseload a provision which was already available to one set of clients, i.e., the elderly, and this view increased its political acceptability. At a time when issues related to children were receiving extensive political attention in Washington, the idea of extending the deduction to families with children had particular political appeal. This stance helped gain the support of conservative members of Congress—particularly Republicans—uncomfortable about voting explicitly for general expansion of an assistance program in the face of the enormous federal deficit. In addition, eliminating the housing deduction would link the proposed

Food Stamp Program changes with efforts to help the homeless—a politically popular focus.

The initial bill introduced by Panetta in the House called for eliminating the cap on the housing deduction by September 30, 1993, and establishing a set of gradually rising transitional caps for the intervening years. In the Senate, both the Sasser/Domenici bill and the Leahy bill also included a staged elimination of the shelter deduction ceiling.

This provision faced very little opposition during the legislative process in the House. Even though it was one of the most expensive provisions of the proposed legislation as originally enacted by the House, it moved through the legislative process with very little discussion.

In the end, however, it became a victim of the budget crisis. After the budget summit meetings in September and October failed to allocate any funds for food stamp program expenditure increases, this provision was deleted from the Leland Act as reported out by the House/Senate Conference Committee with almost no discussion.

AUTHORIZATION FOR STATES TO USE ELECTRONIC BENEFIT TRANSFER SYSTEMS FOR FOOD STAMP ISSUANCE

As discussed in Chapter IV, interest in using electronic benefit transfer (EBT) technology to issue food stamps through client-specific computer accounts has grown in recent years. EBT is more convenient than other issuance systems for both clients and stores, without losing the tie to food purchases and helps reduce fraud and theft, although it has yet to save issuance costs.

The changes in the Food Stamp Program proposed by the Administration in early 1990 included a provision to allow states to adopt EBT systems beginning in 1992, as long as the states could demonstrate that EBT would not increase the costs of administering the program. The stated objective of the Administration in recommending this change was to reduce the fraud and abuse associated with issuing and using food coupons.

As discussions of EBT began in connection with the 1990 legislation, none of the actors took a strong stand against EBT per se. However, whether or not to require that all store check-out lanes in participating stores be equipped with the EBT equipment became a very contentious issue.

The Panetta bill in the House did not directly address whether EBT systems should be authorized on an ongoing basis. However, it did require that *if* any special equipment in stores was used for any "alternative system for the delivery or use of benefits" it was to be operational at *all* registers and checkout lanes. On the Senate side, both the Leahy bill and the Sasser/Domenici bill would have authorized EBT and would have required that all checkout lanes in stores that used EBT have the necessary equipment. The bill introduced by Lugar for the Administration would have allowed EBT without an "all-lanes" requirement.

Client advocacy groups supported the all lanes provisions to prevent the possibility that "second class" check-out lanes would identify, and therefore stigmatize, food stamp participants. Food retailers joined advocacy groups in arguing for preventing discrimination against clients in the stores. But they were also undoubtedly attracted to the possibility that equipment installed at government expense to support EBT could be used by other customers to pay for food purchases using standard checks or debit cards.

The Administration strongly opposed the all lanes requirement on the grounds that it would make EBT more expensive and thus slow its adoption. In the weeks following introduction of the Panetta bill, the administration lobbied both for the explicit authorization of EBT and for dropping the all lanes requirement. The states also opposed the all lanes requirement and lobbied against it, both directly and through the APWA.

During the spring and early summer of 1990, it was clear that an impasse had been reached between the Administration, which strongly opposed the all lanes requirement, and the client advocacy groups and liberal Democrats on the Hill, who believed equally strongly that the requirement was necessary to protect clients. All lanes language remained in the bill reported out of the House Agriculture Committee on July 3 and voted on in the House on August 1. The Administration remained opposed to the requirement.

Later in the summer, USDA took several Hill staff to observe the operations of an EBT demonstration program in Baltimore. Participants in that trip were able to observe an apparently smoothly running EBT system, and several individuals involved with the Leland Act credit this site visit with persuading liberal Democratic staff on the Hill to develop compromise language.

Following that visit, a number of actors, including both Administration and congressional staffers began developing and circulating for review alternative formulations of the lanes requirement. The drafts stopped short of requiring that all lanes be equipped but linked the number of EBT lanes with the volume of a store's food stamp business.

During the late summer, the advocacy groups also voiced some flexibility. While FRAC remained firmly set on requiring all lanes to be equipped for EBT, Robert Greenstein came to the position that clients' interests could be protected with a somewhat less stringent requirement, and he indicated to the Administration a willingness to participate in a compromise that would protect the interests of clients. While no final agreement between Greenstein and the Administration was reached, Greenstein's flexibility on the issue may have helped make additional members of Congress and/or their staffs comfortable with compromise language.

How the all-lanes issue would be treated remained unresolved right up to the series of congressional staff meetings held in mid-October, just before the House/Senate Conference Committee was to focus on the food stamp title of the farm bill. At that time, a compromise position was adopted specifying that EBT-equipped stores in which 15 percent or more of the sales were made with food stamp coupons must have EBT in all checkout lanes. Other stores (the great majority) must offer enough EBT-equipped lanes to ensure that the service provided to food stamp customers is "comparable to the service provided to individuals who are not members of food stamp households," as determined by the Secretary of Agriculture. This compromise was incorporated into the House/Senate Conference Committee report and was subsequently approved by both houses.

CHILD SUPPORT ENFORCEMENT PROVISIONS

The food stamp legislative proposals developed by the Administration in early 1990 and introduced in the Senate by Sen. Lugar would have required that food stamp recipients who needed child support enforcement assistance cooperate with the Child Support Enforcement Program as a condition for receiving food stamps.[7] The Administration strongly supported this proposal during extensive meetings between USDA officials and members of Congress and their staffs, at least in part because additional child support from absent parents would increase household income and thus reduce benefit payments.

The food stamp advocacy groups were strongly opposed to the Administration's proposal. FRAC and the Center on Budget and Policy Priorities felt that the proposal would create another administrative obstacle to program participation. They were also concerned about client confidentiality in cases when program participants had good cause not to cooperate with the Child Support Enforcement Program (for instance, in cases of physical threats by the absent parent). Advocates expressed these concerns in meetings with members of Congress and their staffs and with the Administration. FRAC and CBPP were also joined in these lobbying efforts by a number of advocacy organizations concerned with children's issues including the Children's Defense Fund and the Center for Law and Social Policy.

The proposed child support provisions were also strongly opposed by the APWA, which mobilized state lobbying against the Administration's plans. Much of the APWA's efforts involved targeting senior staff of state human services departments to call their Congressional representatives to express concern about the provisions.

Initial conversations between Administration officials and members of Congress made it clear that many on the Hill shared the advocacy groups' concerns. Congressman Emerson, in particular, urged the Administration to meet with the advocacy groups to work out alternatives that would create safeguards against possible problems and would be acceptable to all parties.

In response, Betty Jo Nelsen, the FNS Administrator, convened a series of meetings between the Administration and the advocacy groups. These meetings led to a proposal put forth by the advocacy groups, under which participation in the Child Support Enforcement Program would have remained voluntary for food stamp recipients, and food stamp agencies would have been required to provide detailed information about the availability of child support enforcement services.

The USDA representatives in the discussions with the advocacy groups tentatively accepted a compromise plan along these lines and agreed to recommend the compromise to other members of the Administration. However, the compromise was vetoed by senior members of the Administration outside USDA, on the grounds that it was not adequately coordinated with the Administration's overall child support enforcement strategies. At this point in the process, USDA withdrew the Administration's proposal altogether. It did so both because it was afraid that continuing to push such legislation after negotiating a compromise would be considered bad faith and because there was little chance that the Hill would pass it.

The advocacy groups had come to favor the compromise and were disappointed to see it fall apart. However, they recognized that the Administration's decision not to accept the compromise was beyond the control of the USDA officials with whom they had been negotiating. In any case, a CSE provision had never been high on their agenda. (They had gone into the legislative process without wanting any CSE provision at all.)[8]

REQUIREMENTS FOR USING AUTOMATED CLIENT DATA BASE SYSTEMS

All states rely heavily on computer-based automated procedures to process data on client households for determining program eligibility and benefit amounts. However, the extent to which particular localities use such methods varies considerably. An issue that received considerable attention during the legislative process leading to the Leland Act was whether or not the federal government should provide additional regulatory and financial incentives to encourage the further application of automated methods in case processing. As discussed below, one unusual factor of the 1990 discussions of this issue, as compared to most other Food Stamp Program issues, is that a representative of a private, for-profit firm, was heavily involved.

As preparations for the 1990 legislative session began, the Electronic Data Systems (EDS) Corporation, a major vendor of computer software systems and data processing services, held discussions with key members of Congress and their staff about the increased case-processing accuracy and efficiency that EDS believed could be achieved with greater automation. EDS's principal representative in these discussions, as noted earlier, was a former congressional staff member who had long been involved in nutrition policy legislation and who now works for a private Washington law firm. To increase the Hill's awareness of the case processing opportunities provided by automation, EDS arranged a demonstration of an advanced client information system, which was set up for members of Congress and their staffs.

Perhaps influenced by these briefings, several members of the House Subcommittee, most importantly Congressman Emerson, the ranking minority member, had become convinced that increased automation was needed in the Food Stamp Program. Reflecting this, the initial Leland Bill submitted in the House encouraged further automation in two primary ways. First, it required the Secretary of Agriculture to develop standards for the initial approval of automation systems, as well as performance standards for ongoing systems reviews. Second, it raised the federal matching rate for state automated system operating costs above its current level of 50 percent.[9] (The exact matching rate level was not specified in the legislation. However, the rate was bounded between 51 and 75 percent.) These

provisions were estimated to have a cost of approximately $25 to
$30 million per year, once they were fully implemented.

The Administration strongly opposed the language in the House
bill, concerned about both the increased costs associated with developing and enforcing additional automation standards and the costs
of the higher reimbursement matching rate. The Administration also
believed that the states were already improving automated procedures at a reasonable rate, and that it would be difficult to develop
standards centrally that would guide the states effectively while still
preserving enough state flexibility to accommodate state variation.

One of the Administration's first steps in attempting to change the
language in the Panetta bill was to meet with EDS to work on an
acceptable compromise. It seemed likely that, if it could have been
achieved, such a compromise would have been acceptable to Congress as well. However, the Administration was not able to strike
a deal with EDS. The Administration's next step was to propose
compromise language to members of Congress and their staffs. In
particular, the Administration proposed legislation that required
reviewing existing standards rather than developing a completely
new set of standards, and dropping the plan to increase the match
rate of systems operating costs.

To support the Administration's arguments that the automation
provisions in the Panetta bill were unnecessary, FNS drew on the
help of its regional offices to develop information on the current
status of automation in the states. The hope was to convince Congress
that advanced automation techniques were being introduced at an
acceptable rate, even without new federal standards. On this issue,
unlike the child support enforcement provisions, the states, as represented by the APWA, were in agreement with the Administration's
position. APWA encouraged its members—particularly those from
states like Vermont with key members on the Agriculture Committees—to contact their representatives and express concern about the
provisions.

The issue and the EDS lobbying placed one of the advocacy groups,
the Food Research and Action Center, in a delicate position. On the
one hand, some members of FRAC were strongly opposed to the
possibility that funds might be diverted from program benefits to a
program administration feature they viewed as of questionable value.
On the other hand, the main lobbyist for EDS was chair of the FRAC
Board of Directors. Throughout the negotiations, he expressed a
strong personal belief that the proposed automation would significantly increase program efficiency.

Another aspect of FRAC's position involved political strategy. Some members of FRAC believed that Emerson was already strongly convinced that the proposed provisions should be kept. These individuals thought that outright opposition to these provisions was not politically useful, as compared to a posture of minimizing the amount of money involved. Overall, the FRAC staff remained split on how to deal with the issue, with some members remaining strongly opposed to the automation provisions.

Robert Greenstein, leader of the other major advocacy group involved in the Leland legislation, was unambiguous in his opposition to the proposed automation provisions. He viewed taking funds from program benefits to support an administrative innovation of unknown usefulness as a travesty, sharing this view with anyone who would listen.

Soon after the Leland legislation was introduced, Greenstein and FRAC staff met with the EDS lobbyist and worked out a tentative deal by which the advocacy groups would not oppose legislative language setting automation standards as long as the standards were flexible, and little or no monies were diverted from the benefit increases proposed in the legislation. This deal broke down, however, for reasons that are not clear.

Initial lobbying attempts by the Administration and the advocacy groups in opposition to the language of the Panetta bill proved largely unsuccessful. The key sections of the proposed automation provisions remained, with only modest changes in the proposed legislation through the committee mark-up process and in the bill enacted by the full House. Nevertheless, the issue remained unresolved—particularly given that the relevant Senators and their staffs were more skeptical than their House counterparts that the automation requirement would be cost-effective. (None of the three bills introduced in the Senate contained the automation provisions.)

In October, lack of funds made the issue moot. Within this context, one of the decisions made at the final set of meetings of Hill staffers was to incorporate into the final bill a watered down automation provision which did not alter the cost matching rate, similar to the compromise language the Administration had suggested early in its discussions with Hill staff members.[10]

What would have happened if the money for a significant program expansion had been found prior to the Conference Committee's deliberations? One view expressed during our interviews is that the original automation language would have remained in the legislation, largely because Bill Emerson remained in favor of it, and his support was central in achieving consensus within the Food Stamp Program policy community for the bill. A different view was that most of the proposed automation language would have been killed, because Robert Greenstein and the states' lobby, including the American Public Welfare Administration, had sufficient influence with the relevant Senate subcommittee members and their staffers to prevent the Senate members of the Conference Committee from accepting it.

It is likely that the final outcome would have depended on the dynamics of what else was going on with the legislation at the time the issue came to a head. Both sides would probably have continued to advance their views on the issue, if the proposed language had remained on the table, but it is unlikely that either of them would have "gone to the wall" on it. At some point, one or the other would probably have backed off, possibly as part of a trade for something else, in order to preserve the overall consensus on the more important parts of the legislation. One likely outcome would have been to adopt some version of the preliminary compromise between the advocacy groups and EDS that had broken down earlier.

AN ASSESSMENT OF THE LEGISLATIVE PROCESS THAT DETERMINES FOOD STAMP POLICY

At the beginning of this chapter, we posed five questions about the legislative process through which food stamp policy is set:

■ What are the underlying forces that lead to food stamp program legislation?
■ Who are the effective decisionmakers in the process?
■ What accounts for the consistently strong political support for the program?
■ Is the legislative process for setting food stamp policy an efficient one?
■ What are the implications for the well-being of the poor of placing jurisdiction for the program with the House and Senate Agriculture Committees?

This section draws on the material in this and in earlier chapters to address these questions.

What Are the Underlying Forces that Lead to Food Stamp Legislation?

In many years no food stamp legislation is seriously proposed. In other years broad consensus emerges that new legislation will be passed. What makes the difference?

- Changes in perceived need
- Changes in political climate
- Technical program administration issues
- Changes in federal budget constraints

Changes in Perceived Need. In the past 15 years, reports in the news media about persons who cannot buy enough food, and about increased use of private food assistance programs, such as soup kitchens and food pantries, have been increasing. Media reports about increasing homelessness have also pointed to a need for more food assistance. Taken together, these factors created a climate of opinion, both in the overall American public and in Congress, that was receptive to proposals to expand food assistance during the latter part of the 1980s.

Changes in the Political Climate. In any year when legislation affecting the Food Stamp Program is enacted, the substance of the legislation reflects the relative balance of power between legislators who want to expand the program and those who do not. Shifts in this balance of power over time may trigger new legislation, altering the parameters of the program. For instance, the legislation enacted in the early 1980s clearly reflected the conservative shift in American politics signaled by the election of Ronald Reagan as president in 1980.

Technical Issues. Food stamp legislation may also be initiated because of technical issues related to program administration. This has been the case particularly with issues relating to program accuracy. As discussed in Chapter IV, legislation was enacted early in the 1980s to strengthen the quality control process in the Food Stamp Program because of concern over high program error rates. Legislation enacted later in the decade reflected a need to correct components of the strengthened quality control system that had been found unworkable.

Federal Budget Constraints. As noted above, within the executive branch of the government, USDA develops food stamp policy initiatives that correspond to budget targets set by OMB. On the legislative side, the relevant congressional subcommittees have, in recent years, attempted to keep program spending within budget targets developed by the House and Senate Budget Committees. Budget constraints were an important force behind the series of legislated program changes in the early 1980s aimed at reducing food stamp benefits, and contributed to limiting the size of the expansionary changes made in the latter half of the 1980s.

Who Are the Effective Decisionmakers?

Food stamp legislation is the product of interactions among members of Congress and their staffs, members of the Administration, client advocacy groups, and several other interested groups. The highly interactive nature of the process makes it generally impossible to attribute specific outcomes to specific participants, but certain generalizations can be made.

RELATIVELY FEW PERSONS ARE INVOLVED DIRECTLY IN DEVELOPING NEW FOOD STAMP LEGISLATION

In a typical year when significant Food Stamp Program legislation is being considered, fewer than 30 persons have detailed knowledge of all aspects of the technical content of the legislation (although others may know the details of specific sections). This number would include 4 to 6 senior staff from the Department of Agriculture and FNS, 6 to 8 congressional staffers (including the staff of the Congressional Research Service and the Congressional Budget Office), 3 to 6 members of Congress, 3 to 5 staff members of advocacy groups, and 2 to 4 staff members from other interest groups. The composition of this group changes over time, but it is stable enough that most members of the group know one another and have had considerable experience in working together. This small number is due in part to the highly technical nature of food stamp legislation. Developing expertise in the Food Stamp Program requires a substantial investment of time, and relatively few persons other than those involved directly in the food stamp legislative process choose to make that investment. It is likely that similarly small numbers of individuals are associated with specialized legislation affecting many other highly technical programs as well.[11]

In describing how they make decisions about legislation, participants in the process often speak of the importance of assessing the types of changes that are "in the air" at the time. Although external forces are obviously relevant, this phrase usually refers to the perceptions of this small group, measured and calibrated through multiple conversations.

Their relatively small number means that members of this group—particularly chairs of the relevant committees and subcommittees—have substantial power in determining not only whether food stamp legislation will be enacted in any given year but also its content. Ultimately, they are afforded such power because their congressional colleagues look to their expertise for leadership in the relevant issues and rarely mount a serious challenge to their decisions. From a longer perspective, of course, their power is significantly constrained by the force of external political pressures.

THE POOR ARE WELL REPRESENTED THROUGH THE POWER OF THE ADVOCACY GROUPS

It has been argued that the poor are not well represented in the political process, because they do not have sufficient resources to hire lobbyists to represent them or to gain access to members of Congress. The food stamp legislative process in the 1980s and early 1990s suggests that client advocacy groups have extensive access to members of Congress and their staffs, and have the interests of those clients well in mind. Using financial support made available by liberal philanthropic foundations and corporations, these groups have been able to develop extensive technical expertise in matters related to the Food Stamp Program and to use that expertise effectively to influence the legislative process in the interests of the needy.

To be sure, they do not have the resources to make significant contributions to political campaigns or to develop major advertising campaigns. Nevertheless, their expertise, reputations for credibility, *and access* make them important contributors to food stamp policy.

We are not arguing that the client advocacy groups always prevail. Obviously they were not able to ensure passage of the program expansions considered during 1990. Nor were they able to prevent the program cuts made in the early Reagan years. On the contrary, the advocacy groups often find themselves in positions where they choose to concede or back off from an issue, to avoid jeopardizing their access to the decisionmaking process in the future. Rather, we are arguing that the needs of the poor are strongly represented and articulated throughout the legislative process, because the client advocates have considerable ability to influence the process.

To be sure, the overall directions taken by welfare policy, including food stamps, are set within a wider arena than the one in which the food stamp in-group functions. But within their more limited context, the advocacy groups appear to have as much ability to shape and influence food stamp legislation as many of their counterparts in the Congress or the Administration.

The 1990 experience also suggests that the advocacy groups are more successful in some parts of the political process than in others. They are particularly effective in working within the specialized committees, where their access and high degree of technical knowledge can be used to greatest advantage. The advocates were much less effective in such broader legislative contexts as the Budget Committees and the Budget Summit process.

THE IMPORTANCE OF TECHNICAL EXPERTISE

As discussed in Chapter II, the rules for determining household eligibility and benefit levels under the program are very complicated. In part they reflect the complexities of developing any assistance program that must serve a broad cross-section of the poor. In part they reflect the further complications introduced by the program's links to food consumption. And in part they reflect the decision to specify detailed eligibility and benefit rules at the federal level.

During the past decade, in particular, little has been left to administrative discretion. The resulting complexity of decisions made at the federal legislative level require investments of substantial time to understand exactly how the program works and the likely effects of proposed changes. Such complexity tends to shift the balance of power in the political processes toward technical experts, at least until the going gets rough on overall budget constraints. In addition, it provides a mechanism through which advocacy groups can gain access to decisionmakers.

Technical expertise over this period has been very important in providing political cover for expanding benefits more, or contracting them less, than Food Stamp Program advocates would have been able to do if they had used the rhetoric of benefit expansion. The Mickey Leland experience demonstrates the limits of this tactic.

THE BIPARTISAN NATURE OF RECENT FOOD STAMP LEGISLATION

Another prominent feature of the food stamp legislative process that affects the locus of decisionmaking is that much of the legislation passed in recent years has had relatively little opposition. In recent

years, for instance, legislation has frequently been introduced jo.
by the chairs and minority leaders of the relevant committees or
subcommittees, and final legislation both in the Senate and House
of Representatives has often been passed by large majorities. The
high value placed on consensual decisionmaking by most members
of the food stamp policy community, particularly the relevant members of Congress and their staffs, tends to blur any analysis of who
the effective decision makers in the process are. Most of the actors
have considerable power to press any individual provision about
which they feel very strongly. However, at the same time, they must
be prepared to "give" on most issues in order to reach final agreement
on the overall package.

The degree of consensus in the food stamp legislative decision
process, in our judgment, has maximized political support for the
program from the Congress as a whole, since the inside members of
the policy setting community present a united front to other legislators. Also, the high premium placed on consensus allows all members
of this community to get at least some of what they want out of the
process (in order to keep them from blocking the consensus everyone
wants).

A negative aspect of decisionmaking through consensus by a small
and stable set of persons is its potential to limit the likelihood of
new ideas and perspectives being seriously considered, thus inhibiting major program changes. Indeed, the stability of the structure of
the Food Stamp Program since the 1977 legislation provides evidence
of this. However, in assessing the magnitude of this risk, it is important to remember that structural change per se is not necessarily a
good thing. The degree to which major change is desirable depends
importantly on one's assessment as to how well a program is meeting
its objectives, an issue we discuss in the last chapter.

What Accounts for the Consistently Strong Political Support Enjoyed by the Food Stamp Program?

Although the Food Stamp Program has changed frequently since
1977, the changes have been relatively small. The cuts and later
increases in maximum benefit levels (in constant dollar terms) that
were enacted between 1981 and 1990 were all within 7 percentage
points of the maximum benefit levels at the start of the decade.
Changes in the earned income deduction during the 1980s reduced
the percentage of earnings deducted from gross income from 20 to
18 percent and later restored the 20 percent figure.

No changes affecting the basic structure of the program have been enacted since elimination of the food stamp purchase requirement in the Food Stamp Act of 1977. The basic structure of the program seems to have been widely accepted, with liberals and conservatives engaging in repeated skirmishes over specific program parameters that have led to relatively small movements in one direction or another—depending on the political strength of the different actors, on budgetary tightness, and on media reports highlighting need.

What accounts for this ongoing political support? Two factors already discussed—the emotional strength of the hunger issue and the fact that food stamp benefits are specifically linked to food— are very important. Even though the program's direct links to food consumption have been weakened over time—most importantly, because the purchase requirement was eliminated in 1977—the perceived links generate a broad reservoir of support, both within the Congress and in the general public, which can be tapped for political support.

A third factor that appears to generate crucial congressional support is the general perception that the program is working efficiently. Members of Congress and their staffs who examine the Food Stamp Program closely find that, despite flaws, it is successful at transferring public assistance benefits to a large number of households who need assistance. It is also important that the program serves a very broad constituency, including families with children, the elderly, and disabled and many working poor households (Greenstein, 1991).

When asked to explain why food stamp legislation is so often proposed and enacted on a bipartisan basis with a large margin of support, many participants in the legislative process point out that many of the key members of Congress in this area, including Panetta, Emerson, and Leahy, are "reasonable" persons whose style is consensus-building rather than confrontation. There is no doubt that personal styles play a role—the process was considerably less bipartisan in the early 1980s when Jesse Helms was the chair of the relevant Senate committee. Even then, however, bipartisan support for the Food Stamp Program was considerable, reflecting its broad appeal to widely varying constituencies.

Implications of Legislative Jurisdiction in the Agriculture Committees

As noted earlier, placement of legislative responsibility for the Food Stamp Program with the House and Senate Agriculture Committees sets it apart from most other benefit programs. Given that it is now America's largest means-tested income assistance program, why is responsibility for it still located in committees concerned with agricultural markets rather than social policy? Should this historical accident be changed in order to enhance legislative efficiency, or are social purposes served by the current arrangement?

Separate legislative responsibility is clearly inefficient in that it impedes coordination of program rules among the different components of the U.S. welfare system. For instance, there are differences in income and household composition definitions and work requirements used in determining benefits between the Food Stamp Program and other assistance programs such as AFDC. Since the Food Stamp Program and other assistance programs are often administered jointly at the state and local levels, even small differences in key program rules can lead to inefficiencies in program administration. Some of these discrepancies reflect different program objectives, but often the differences reflect nothing more than arbitrary choices between equally attractive alternatives made in different ways by different committees at different times.

Splitting legislative jurisdiction can also lead to odd tradeoffs. Rather than balancing the relative advantages of alternative income maintenance programs when facing budget constraints, for example, the Agriculture Committees must often trade off food stamp benefits against agricultural price supports and other issues having nothing to do with income assistance.

Under the current system, only at the level of the full House or the full Senate can choices between food stamps and other assistance programs be made, and the choices at this level are heavily constrained by decisions already made at the committee level, except when overall budget constraints are made effective. A seemingly more rational arrangement would be a "welfare committee" that balances the merits of public assistance alternatives and an agriculture committee that considers alternative agricultural policies, reserving for the full houses the task of balancing the two sets of recommendations.

A related disadvantage of the current split is that the types of expertise relevant to analyzing Food Stamp Program issues are quite different from those relevant for dealing with agricultural policies. This almost certainly leads to duplication of committee staff expertise.

But yet another tradeoff is relevant here—between legislative efficiency and political support. For the latter, there may be advantages in housing jurisdiction with the Agriculture Committees. Garnering support for the program from agricultural interests gives it a wider political base. While we know of no recent explicit deals in which support for other agriculture programs was traded for support for the Food Stamp Program, placing its jurisdiction in the Agriculture committees creates a context for implicit tradeoffs. Also, including the Food Stamp Program in the same legislation that provides support for agriculture markets widens support for the program on the floors of the two houses. In addition, assigning the program to the Agriculture Committees helps preserve the rationale for the in-kind nature of its benefits, which also helps ensure popular support for the program.

In our judgment, if jurisdiction over the program were transferred to the committees that oversee the other major U.S. cash assistance programs—most notably AFDC—the pressures to convert food stamps to cash benefits and to integrate them with the other programs would prove insurmountable. The separate identity of the Food Stamp Program would be lost, and it is likely that over time this would lead to an erosion of the total resources available to the poor. Our argument is that the in-kind nature of the program is essential for its support, and that keeping jurisdiction within the Agriculture Committees is part of what preserves the use of in-kind benefits.

Is the Food Stamp Legislation Process Efficient?

Three key issues reflect on whether the food stamp legislative process is efficient: Are the heavy commitments of participants' time necessary? Are the dynamics through which decisions are made productive? Is the frequency with which program changes have been legislated efficient?

THE HEAVY COMMITMENT OF PARTICIPANTS' TIME REQUIRED IN THE LEGISLATIVE PROCESS

As illustrated by our case study of the Leland Act, the food stamp policy legislative process places heavy time demands on many people. Members of Congress, congressional staff members, senior officials of the Department of Agriculture, advocacy group representatives, and representatives of other interest groups all devoted extensive amounts of time to developing the 1990 legislation, which ended up being considerably less ambitious than the versions on which so much time was expended. These time commitments are typical of other years when major food stamp legislation has been passed without such truncation.

This calls into question whether or not the legislative process for setting food stamp policy is an efficient one. At first glance, the process would appear to be very inefficient in time use. During the process that led up to the Leland Act, for example, much time was spent in repeated discussions and negotiations among participants in the process, talking and then talking again about the relatively small set of substantive policy issues being considered. Is there not a more efficient way to achieve the best possible legislation within the political constraints of the period? Probably not.

Because of the many constituencies involved and the complicated nature of the Food Stamp Program, the extensive discussions described above were probably necessary to forge a bill which reflected a broad set of interests. In the end, of course, many of these discussions became moot when it turned out that no additional funding for the program was made available. But at the outset, nobody involved knew that this would happen (indeed, most expected a very different outcome), and it was important that the process be ready with a fully thought-out bill, if funding became available.

It was obviously inefficient, with hindsight, to have such extensive discussions of provisions that were ultimately cut from the bill. However, posing the above question from the perspective of full knowledge of the eventual outcome of the legislation presents too stringent a test. Given the information available in early 1990, it was reasonable to believe that a substantial food stamp bill would be passed, and the discussions among key actors helped ensure that, if passed, the bill would be a good one. Similar processes led to passage of significant food stamp bills in 1985 and 1988. This suggests that the considerable wasted effort in 1990 is not a symptom of overall inefficiency in the food stamp legislative process as much as evidence of an occasional "bad year."[12]

Finally, it is useful to note that, when examined in the context of the overall size of the Food Stamp Program, the amount of resources invested in the legislative process is relatively small. As detailed above, the amount of time involved in the process was at most a few months for each of a small number of key actors. This is a small effort if it results in even a very modest increase in the effectiveness of a program which spends more than $25 billion annually.

THE FINAL DECISION PROCESS FOR THE LELAND ACT

As already described, many of the final decisions about the Leland Act were made during two very long meetings attended by legislative staff and USDA officials. These meetings were conducted under very tight time pressures until late at night, since closure had to be reached on all relevant issues before the farm bill conference committee began considering the nutrition title of the bill.

On the face of it, making significant program decisions at 2:00 A.M. under intense time pressure would appear to be a risky procedure, and, to some degree, it probably was. However, it is important to note that the issues dealt with at these final meetings were ones that had been considered extensively over the previous nine months of discussion and negotiation.

The fact that the specific policy alternatives that were "on the table" had been discussed extensively in the preceding months limited potential errors due to the time pressures and group dynamics of the final meetings. Thus, while 2:00 A.M. is not the ideal time to make decisions about an important public program, the risks of serious mistakes were certainly smaller than a similar process that did not build on extensive prior discussion.

THE LEVEL OF DETAIL CONTAINED IN FOOD STAMP LEGISLATION

As illustrated by the Leland bill, one striking aspect of Food Stamp Program legislation in the past 20 years has been the high level of detail with which it specifies program procedures. Very little is left to regulatory decisions. This has not always been the case. During the 1960s and early 1970s, the food stamp authorizing legislation left considerable room for administrative discretion. Indeed, the Food Stamp Program during that period has been used as the basis for a case study of how policy can be developed through administrative rules rather than legislation (Berry, 1984).

It was during the Nixon Administration in the 1970s, that Congress began to enact food stamp legislation containing a high level of detail. Several factors appear to be responsible for this. In part, it reflects a belief by Congress that both the Administration and the courts ignored congressional intent in dealing with food stamp issues in the late 1960s and early 1970s (Melnick, forthcoming). In part, it reflects increasing sophistication among participants in the legislative process. As individuals from various points in the political spectrum have become more knowledgeable about the technical issues associated with structuring and operating the program, they use their technical knowledge increasingly to advance their positions in legislative policy debates. The result of this has been very detailed, highly technical, legislation.

Another factor explaining the technical complexity of the program is the importance which many legislators and advocates place on it as a central component of America's overall "safety net" for assisting the poor. The program's role as the only national program available to essentially all poor households is seen as making it particularly important that there be detailed program rules to ensure that it is being carried out according to Congressional intent.

FREQUENT LEGISLATIVE CHANGES IN THE PROGRAM

Another aspect of food stamp legislative decisionmaking that affects the efficiency of the process is the frequency with which legislative changes have been made to the program during the past decade. Although the basic structure of the program was not changed, Food Stamp Program legislation was passed in five of the years between 1980 and 1989, including several direct reversals of policy. As noted, changes in maximum benefit levels and the earned income deduction made in 1981 and 1982 legislation were largely reversed by legislation passed in the latter half of the decade. And, administrative changes in quality control and monthly reporting in the early 1980s were reversed in later years.

These frequent changes in the program can be attributed to, in large degree, such factors as changes in the federal budget and the shifting balance of political power. In addition, particularly with changes in administration procedures, there has been an element of "trial and error" in the process, whereby changes have first been made and then later modified, based on lessons learned.

The frequent changes to the program reflect the responsiveness of the process, both to perceived changes in economic and social conditions and to changes in political priorities. But in several ways the process has been *too* responsive. In particular, the very frequent changes have been inefficient, due both to the legislative time required by these bills and to the high state and local costs of constantly having to adjust program rules and procedures to reflect changes in federal legislation.

During the early and mid-1980s, when food stamp legislation was changing particularly often, one of the most common complaints made by state and local administrators was that the constantly changing rules made it impossible to operate the program effectively. In particular, because of the necessity to retrain staff and modify computer systems, these changes were perceived as leading both to high error rates and to high administrative costs—costs that the legislators in Washington did not fully understand. It is certainly arguable that the same long-term results could have been achieved at lower cost had the legislative system been somewhat *less* sensitive to political changes.

Notes

1. This chapter draws heavily on personal interviews of persons involved in the process leading up to the 1990 food stamp legislation. About 20 interviews were conducted by the authors during the spring and summer of 1991 with legislative staff members, officials of the U.S. Department of Agriculture, and representatives of advocacy groups and other private organizations involved in the legislative process. Most of the information reported in the text about events and positions held by various actors was obtained from these interviews.

2. For an additional discussion of the political and environmental factors that shape Food Stamp Program policy, see R. Shep Melnick's forthcoming book, provisionally titled: *The Politics of Statutory Rights: Courts and the Congress in the Welfare State.* Other useful analyses of the politics of food stamps are provided in Berry (1984) and Maney (1989).

3. EBT systems are described and discussed in more detail in Chapter IV.

4. Under separate regulations, FNS cannot require stores to pay for the cost of the equipment, so this would have involved government provision of the equipment.

5. This judgment is based on interviews with key staff. See also Kosterlitz (1990) for a discussion of the expectation by members of the relevant policy community as of this point in the process that significant expansionary food stamp legislation would be passed.

6. The increase in annual food stamp benefits resulting from the provision once it was fully in effect was estimated to be more than half a billion dollars (U.S. Congress, House of Representatives, Committee on Agriculture, 1990, p. 906).

7. A similar provision is already included in the AFDC program.

8. The text discussion focuses only on one of two proposed Leland Act provisions on child support enforcement. The other proposed provision, which is not discussed in the text, is language included in the original Panetta bill which would have disregarded the first $50 of child support payments received when income is computed for food stamp purposes. This provision, whose purpose was to provide custodial parents with financial incentives for cooperating with the Child Support Enforcement Program, would have made the food stamp treatment of child support parallel with the treatment of child support in the AFDC program. Support for this proposal, both within Congress and among many of the special interest groups, was considerable. It was dropped for cost reasons.

9. The proposed language would have applied to *operating* costs. The matching rate for *development and installation* costs for automated systems has been set at 75 percent for some time.

10. This was somewhat ironic, since the Administration would have preferred that the bill not contain any automation provision and might well have achieved its full objectives if the compromise language had not been on the table. However, at the time

the Administration developed the compromise language, it had no way of knowing that budget constraints would come to its aid.

11. The high levels of congressional specialization and expertise associated with the Food Stamp Program have also been noted with regard to other programs as well. See, for instance, Davidson and Olezek (1985), p. 359.

12. Whether the broader political process that resulted in the inaccurate deficit projections and the continuing budget uncertainty during the spring and summer of 1990 is efficient is a very different question that goes way beyond the scope of our analysis.

Chapter Eight

CONCLUSIONS AND POLICY RECOMMENDATIONS

Throughout the book, we have highlighted the key policy tradeoffs encountered in designing and operating an income maintenance program. In this concluding chapter, we discuss our conclusions regarding those tradeoffs and our policy recommendations concerning the future of the Food Stamp Program.

KEY POLICY TRADEOFFS

Seven policy tradeoffs associated with income maintenance programs were highlighted in Chapter I:

- Benefit targeting versus program access
- Benefit adequacy versus available resources
- Program accuracy versus program access and costs
- Access to the program versus administrative costs
- In-kind benefits versus administrative costs and recipient needs
- Work incentives versus costs and access to the program
- State and local flexibility versus other program goals

Benefit Targeting versus Access

The Food Stamp Program is highly successful at targeting its benefits to those most in need of them. More than 91 percent of food stamp recipient households have incomes below the U.S.-defined poverty levels according to 1991 administrative data, and most of the remainder are households near the poverty cutoff level with disabled or elderly members.

However, this highly successful targeting has come at the expense of a great deal of program complexity. As reviewed in Chapter II, the rules for determining program eligibility and benefit levels are exceedingly complicated, and require that applicants supply extensive information about income receipts and living arrangements.

This complexity, in turn, reduces access for eligible households who are unable or unwilling to comply with program requirements. This problem applies to all potential client groups, but it is most serious for populations with particular problems complying with complicated procedural requirements, such as the frail elderly and the homeless. Program complexity also raises operational costs and increases error rates.

In our judgement, simplifying program benefit eligibility and benefit determination rules to reduce program complexity is urgently needed even if this somewhat reduces the program's ability to precisely target benefits. It is also important to develop more successful ways of meeting the nutrition needs of vulnerable groups, such as the frail elderly and the homeless, either by giving them special assistance in coping with administrative requirements or by assuring their access to other nutrition assistance programs designed especially to serve them.

The Adequacy of Benefits versus Available Resources

As reviewed in Chapter III, the adequacy of food stamp benefits can be viewed from two perspectives, reflecting the joint role of the program in the American income maintenance system. The narrow program goal is to ensure that eligible households have access to sufficient food to provide them with healthy diets, without having to spend inordinate proportions of their income on food. Judged against this objective, the Food Stamp Program benefit levels, with their basis in the Thrifty Food Program, are reasonably successful in accomplishing the program's objective for participating households.

However, because the Food Stamp Program is one of the largest federally funded components of America's income maintenance system and is the only U.S. assistance program that is widely available without categorical restrictions, it is also reasonable to ask whether the program, in conjunction with other parts of the system, is successful in lifting low-income Americans out of poverty. As described in Chapter III, neither the current food stamp benefit levels nor the available cash welfare assistance programs raise many food stamp households out of poverty. While the program provides extensive and much needed assistance in alleviating the effects of poverty for millions of American households, only about 15 percent of program households are raised out of poverty by the combination of cash assistance, earnings, and food stamps.

If America is to eliminate poverty, benefit levels under the Food Stamp Program and other components of the income maintenance system must be expanded. Whether benefit expansion receives high priority in the context of concerns about the federal deficit will be decided through the political process. We believe that it should.

Program Accuracy versus Program Access and Costs

The heavy emphasis on lowering the program error rates in the mid-1980s produced standards that the administering agencies could not meet. States were being held to error rate standards that many claimed were impossible. This led agencies and their staff to require extensive and burdensome documentation from clients and to be overly conservative in determining eligibility for benefits.

The revised QC structure created by the Hunger Prevention Act of 1988 appears to have been successful in redressing this balance. Program error rates are continuing to decline or hold steady, while the pressures on front-line staff have been reduced. No further major adjustments to the overall QC System appear needed. However, it is important that states with relatively high error rates continue to work on ways of improving program accuracy, through improved staff training, increased staff support through automation, and improved cross-checking of information against external computerized sources.

Access versus Administrative Costs

For many clients, access to the Food Stamp Program is not convenient or timely. As cited in Chapter III, a recent General Accounting Office report found that many eligible households are not participating because of administrative requirements and difficulty in physically getting to a food stamp office. In addition, the evidence presented in Chapter IV suggests that in many instances, legislated timeliness standards are not being met, either for regular clients (who are to be served within 30 days) or for "expedited services" cases (which are to be processed within 5 days). This evidence suggests that the Food Stamp Program may, in many parts of the country, be providing too few administrative resources to ensure adequate access to the program. Attention should be given to developing ways of more effectively enforcing federal standards in these areas.

In-Kind Benefits versus Administrative Costs and Recipient Needs

The current use of food coupons rather than cash as the form of benefit ensures that benefits are spent largely on food. However, coupons are inconvenient for both stores and clients, and significantly add to program administrative costs. In light of this, there is substantial interest in cash-out, under which program benefits would be distributed in the form of checks rather than coupons.

While there would clearly be administrative advantages to switching to cash-out, the available evidence on food expenditures, as reviewed in Chapter V, suggests that switching to the use of checks would lead to a reduction in the food expenditures of the average food stamp household.

Perhaps more important, it is likely that switching to checks would incur substantial political costs. The political history of the Food Stamp Program suggests that the program's direct links to reducing hunger have been an important source of political support. As summarized in Chapter VII, there is strong evidence that the public is more comfortable transferring assistance in the form of food coupons as opposed to providing assistance as cash benefits. In light of this, a switch away from coupons could significantly erode public support for the program. Indeed, it might well end the program as a separate entity.

If the full value of the benefits now received as food coupons could be combined with other assistance programs into a more integrated system, some would not mourn the loss of the Food Stamp Program per se. The danger is that eliminating coupons would lead to cuts in the assistance package as a whole, because public support for food coupons is **not** translatable into public support for cash assistance.

In any event, advancing technology may make the cash-out debate moot. As debit and credit cards become increasingly commonplace for food purchases made by the non-assistance population, electronic benefit transfer (EBT) systems for food stamps are likely to become increasingly cost effective. Since EBT systems can provide many of the advantages of cash-out without giving up the linkages to food, they are likely to be a more promising policy alternative than cash-out in the future.

Work Incentives versus Costs and Access

Reducing dependence on welfare programs is a major public policy objective. But maintaining incentives to work inevitably conflicts with the goals of constraining costs and targeting benefits to the most needy, as discussed in Chapter II. Furthermore, there are serous concerns about the effectiveness of the current Food Stamp Employment and Training Program, as discussed in Chapter VI.

We believe a reasonable balance has been struck between maintaining a low program benefit reduction rate to encourage work effort and constraining costs and keeping benefits focused on the most needy. Although cumulative tax rates for recipients receiving benefits from multiple programs such as AFDC and Food Stamps are often very high, reductions of as much as ten percentage points in the Food Stamp Program benefit reduction rate would probably increase work by only a small amount, while eroding the program's ability to target benefits on the most needy.

The minimal impacts of the Food Stamp Employment and Training Program almost certainly reflect its low funding and the fact that it is only one of several employment and training programs directed at low-wage workers. Therefore, policy alternatives that should be considered include either spending more per participant on E&T services or discontinuing the program. Spending more per participant could be accomplished under current funding by concentrating E&T services on a narrower portion of the food stamp population. Alternatively, funding could be increased. But options that spend more per participant should incorporate rigorous evaluations of the impacts of the E&T program. If there is still no effect, there is no defensible reason, in our judgement, to continue the E&T services in a world of scarce benefit resources.

State and Local Flexibility versus Other Goals: The Issue of Block Grants

One alternative to the current structure of the Food Stamp Program which was actually approved by the Senate Agriculture Committee in 1982 would create nutritional "block grants" to the states.[1] Under this plan, the federal funds currently allocated to the Food Stamp Program (and perhaps those allocated to some other federal nutrition programs, as well) would be distributed to the states. States would be expected to use the funds for nutrition-related activities but would be given wide latitude in how to provide such assistance.

This type of proposal highlights the tradeoff discussed earlier between the flexibility of state and local control versus the accomplishment of federal objectives. One potential advantage of a block grant system is that states could structure nutrition assistance to be fully compatible with their administrative environments. For instance, the state of Alabama recently obtained a set of waivers of federal Food Stamp Program requirements in order to set up its ASSETS demonstration, under which it is integrating several low-income assistance programs.

Converting the Food Stamp Program to a block grant would also allow states more room for local choice in targeting benefits. For instance, if a state judged that, in its population, the frail elderly were at particular nutritional risk, a nutritional block grant program would make it possible for the state to divert funds currently used for food stamps into a strengthened "meals on wheels" program. Under the current Food Stamp Program, the states cannot make such choices.

The possible advantages, however, become potential disadvantages when viewed from a different perspective. Giving states *more choice* gives the federal government *less control*. To the extent that nutritional assistance is viewed as a national program, it is appropriate and important for the federal government to be setting standards as to who will be served by the program and how they should be served. State flexibility would undercut this.

The danger is illustrated by the AFDC program, under which states are given substantial flexibility. In AFDC, failure to set federal standards for benefit levels has resulted in large benefit differences among states. For instance, the 90th percentile state in terms of benefits (Connecticut) has a maximum benefit for a family of three that is over 300 percent higher than that in the 10th percentile state (Louisiana).[2] In our view, this wide range of benefits is totally inappropriate. Moving food stamp benefits in that direction would further limit the ability of the federal government to ensure minimally decent living standards.

Posed in this way, the issue becomes a value judgement regarding which level of government should have the responsibility for dealing with poverty. Our own view is that alleviating poverty in America and ensuring adequate nutritional standards for Americans are *national* goals. It is, therefore, highly appropriate for the federal government to be in charge of meeting these goals uniformly in the various states.

The force of our argument is strengthened when we consider other possible implications of block grants. Despite the rhetoric of local control, calls for block grants are often thinly disguised attempts to reduce the resources devoted to income assistance policies over time. The current structure of the Food Stamp Program as a federal entitlement, and the fact that the program is indexed for inflation, unlike

AFDC, imply that the program expands and contracts automatically as the need for it varies. Under most block grant proposals the funds allocated would be fixed, with no price indexing and no federally mandated entitlement for eligible persons.

As a result, under a block grant system, program funds would almost certainly rise less than they will with the current program structure. Nor would they rise to meet the need of workers laid off during economic downturns. To be sure, Congress could increase the size of the block grants from time to time and such grants could even be directly indexed. But the political reality is that increases would be less likely. This is illustrated by the experience of the Food Stamp Program in Puerto Rico, which was converted to a block grant in 1982. Between 1983 and 1992, the funds allocated to the block grant program increased 23 percent, compared to 88 percent growth in federal expenditures on the regular Food Stamp Program in the 50 states, the District of Columbia, the Virgin Islands, and Guam. (U.S. Congress, House of Representatives, Committee on Ways and Means, 1992 and data supplied by FNS).

IS MORE INTEGRATION OF ASSISTANCE PROGRAMS DESIRABLE?

As noted in Chapter I, the American public assistance system is composed of a substantial number of individual programs that have evolved independently, are operated separately, and are under the jurisdiction of several different congressional committees. On the face of it, this grossly inefficient arrangement raises the question of whether more integration is desirable.

We believe that, modest additional program integration is useful and feasible, but that there are significant drawbacks to any far-reaching movement toward assistance program integration. We discuss these issues at two levels:

■ Should the Food Stamp Program be more integrated with AFDC?
■ Should all low-income assistance programs in the United States be integrated?

Integration of Food Stamps and AFDC

Issues relating to integrating the AFDC and Food Stamp Programs warrant special attention because of the high degree of overlap in the target populations. Past discussions of program integration have frequently focused on these two programs.

CURRENT DEGREE OF INTEGRATION

There is already considerable integration at the local level in the administration of the AFDC and Food Stamp Programs for households eligible for both types of assistance. The Hunger Prevention Act of 1988 requires that states allow applicants to submit a single application for both food stamps and AFDC (unless the states meet certain exception rules), and in most parts of the country the same case worker serves both the AFDC and the food stamp case for a household participating in both programs. Also, the rules defining income and assets for program eligibility and benefit determination are similar, though not the same, for the two programs.

Some inconsistencies between AFDC and food stamps impede efficient administration, however. For instance, certain types of income are treated differently, such as federal education (Pell) grants, which may be countable income under the Food Stamp Program but not under AFDC. The methods of measuring the countable value of cars and other vehicles in determining assets also vary substantially between the two programs.

These discrepancies mean that different information on income and assets has to be obtained from the client when processing applications for the two programs. Furthermore, once this information is collected, the rules for determining net income and net assets, as well as those for determining benefits, are completely different for the two programs, so that separate benefit determination calculations have to be made.

PARTIAL INTEGRATION OF AFDC AND FOOD STAMPS

There is no question that there should be some additional integration of the AFDC and Food Stamp Programs. No purpose is served, for instance, by discrepancies in the ways income and assets are calculated under the two programs. Eliminating these discrepancies would make it possible to streamline program operations at the local level, thus reducing administrative costs.

Somewhat more problematic is whether to achieve more conformity in the benefit calculation formulas used in the two programs. Currently, the AFDC program leaves to the states considerable discretion not only in the level of AFDC payments but also in how they are calculated. Attempting to integrate benefit formulas across the programs would require (1) reducing the flexibility of states in operating the AFDC program or (2) moving away from national uniformity in the operating of the Food Stamp Program. We believe that the first of these possibilities, increased uniformity in the AFDC program, is desirable, but not likely politically, while the second alternative poses grave risks for the well-being of the poor.

In any case, additional integration of AFDC and food stamps is not likely to save large amounts of administrative costs. There is already substantial integration in how the programs are actually administered at the local level, and computers are being used increasingly to implement the different calculations necessary under the two programs. Also, experienced case workers are already adept at moving from AFDC to food stamp rules as needed in serving their clients.

Program integration has become a favorite rhetorical issue with state and federal politicians looking for easy ways to save money without reducing benefits. The hard reality is that the saving from partial program consolidation would not be sufficient to fund meaningful benefit increases.

FULL INTEGRATION OF THE AFDC AND FOOD STAMPS

A broader potential reform would fully combine the AFDC and Food Stamp Programs, including the transfer of federal administrative responsibilities for food stamps from the Department of Agriculture to the Department of Health and Human Services and transfer of congressional oversight from the agriculture committees to the committees which oversee AFDC.

Such integration would simplify program administration, but the cost savings would be modest. The potential gains from consolidating the two programs are limited by the fact that they have significantly different objectives. Most importantly, AFDC's target group is limited to needy households with children, while the Food Stamp Program targets assistance to all low-income households at nutritional risk. As we have seen in previous chapters, well under half of food stamp households also receive AFDC. Therefore, consolidating food stamps with AFDC would require more than just folding the Food Stamp Program into an existing program. The new consolidated program would have to serve many clients AFDC does not now serve. Eliminating the duplicative federal bureaucracies in the Department of Agriculture and the Department of Health and Human Services would produce savings. However, these savings would be limited by the fact that the broader scope of any combined program would require a larger bureaucracy within the Department of Health and Human Services than is now needed for AFDC.

At the local level, the points made in the previous section concerning partial program integration apply as well to full program integration. The reality is that the two programs are already integrated in most jurisdictions. Thus, the gains from further integration are limited.

The greatest consequences of AFDC and Food Stamp Program consolidation would be political. As we have stressed earlier, once full consolidation was achieved, we believe the pressure to convert food stamp benefits to cash could not be resisted. Once this was done, the Food Stamp Program would lose its separate identify and its separate constituency—an outcome likely to result in fewer overall resources for means-tested assistance.

General Integration of All U.S. Public Assistance Programs

An alternative to the current public assistance system in America, with its odd combination of multiple but overlapping programs, would be a single consolidated program designed to meet all the objectives of the current system. Such a consolidated program might, for instance, incorporate elements of the Food Stamp Program, AFDC, SSI, the various housing assistance programs, Medicaid, and numerous smaller programs.

From a purely technical point of view, program integration of this sort would be highly desirable in two ways. First, it could serve the poor better by coordinating all the benefits and the application procedures. There would be less likelihood of households being lost in the cracks and unable to deal effectively with multiple bureaucracies. Second, a coordinated system could potentially operate at significantly lower administrative costs. In particular, the need for multiple overlapping bureaucracies at federal, state, and local levels would be eliminated.

Notwithstanding these considerable advantages, however, we believe that the political arguments against consolidation hold here, too. Each of the current programs has its own political constituencies that create support for it, and many involve in-kind benefits. As we have stressed in our discussion of the Food Stamp Program, use of in-kind benefits is very important in mobilizing popular support for low-income assistance—reflecting deeply held attitudes of the American public.

FINAL OBSERVATIONS

It has now been more than 15 years since the current structure of the Food Stamp Program was established through the Food Stamp

Act of 1977, which eliminated the food stamp purchase requirement. Over that period, the Food Stamp Program has become an increasingly major component of America's overall strategy for alleviating the burden of poverty for low-income Americans.

More than 25 million Americans receive food stamps. For most food stamp households, program benefits represent a significant component of their overall purchasing power. Furthermore, program benefits are indexed for inflation; as a result, the levels of benefits for which households are eligible have largely kept up with rising prices.

There have been, and remain, significant limitations to the program. However, as emphasized in earlier chapters, many of these limitations reflect the choices among competing objectives that must be made in the design of any public assistance program. The fundamental message of this book is the importance, when assessing a proposed program change, of considering the *overall* impacts of the proposed change on *multiple* program objectives, rather than focusing on the single dimension the change is designed to improve.

While many changes were made to specific parameters of the Food Stamp Program during the 1980s, most were relatively minor. The basic structure of the Food Stamp Program has been remarkably stable since the 1977 legislation. This stability reflects a broad consensus that ensuring access to adequate nutrition is an important priority for the United States and that, overall, the Food Stamp Program provides a strong basis for accomplishing this objective.

Despite the central role that the Food Stamp Program plays in America's overall income maintenance policies, however, it is important to recognize that the program does not, and was never intended to, meet all the assistance needs of its target population. Because of its focus on food, the program's benefits are not sufficient by themselves to raise most of its participant households out of poverty. The challenge for income maintenance policy in the United States during the 1990s is to successfully combine the Food Stamp Program, other public assistance programs, and employment programs, to ensure that all Americans are able to meet their basic needs.

Notes

1. A variant, which would also have shifted responsibility for nutrition assistance programs to the states, was proposed by President Reagan in his January 1982 State of the Union Address.
2. Data supplied by the U.S. Department of Health and Human Services, Administration for Children and Families.

APPENDICES

COMPARISONS OF PROGRAM DATA AND CURRENT POPULATION SURVEY DATA ON PERCENTAGE OF FOOD STAMP RECIPIENTS ABOVE THE POVERTY LINE

The tabulations of Food Stamp Program data presented in Chapter III suggest that 9 percent of food stamp recipient households have gross incomes above the poverty threshold. However, as noted in that chapter, analyses based on Current Population Survey (CPS) data place this figure considerably higher, at about 27 percent.[1]

Attempting to resolve the discrepancy is of considerable interest, both because the issue itself is important and because it illustrates how the technical program design issues raised in Chapter III can become very important in program assessments. As discussed in this Appendix, three technical factors account in good part for the differences in the estimates obtained from the two data sets on the proportion of food stamp households below poverty: (1) differences in the accounting periods over which income and household composition are measured, (2) differences in the recipient unit definitions, and (3) technical survey issues, including different methods for imputing data for survey item nonresponse. In addition, errors in both the CPS and the available program data probably play a significant role.

ACCOUNTING PERIOD

As noted in Chapter II, the Food Stamp Program uses a single month as its accounting period. However, the reference period used to measure income in official U.S. poverty statistics based on the CPS is the entire previous year. A significant number of households with temporary income losses receive food stamps only for part of the full year covered by the Census data. The monthly incomes of some of these households were below the poverty threshold during their period of food stamp receipt, even though their income for the entire year was high enough to place them above the poverty line.

RECIPIENT UNIT DEFINITION

The recipient unit definition for the Food Stamp Program does not necessarily include all of the persons who reside in the same dwelling unit. The Census statistics on the percentage of poor households that participate in the Food Stamp Program are based on the combined income of all persons in the dwelling unit, without taking into account that the food stamp household may be a subset of the dwelling-unit. Evidence presented in Landa (1987) suggests that many of the households that contain members who are not included in the food stamp recipient unit, can count on these members for a significant amount of earned income. In some cases, the households defined in the Census data have income above the poverty level, even though the food stamp recipient units on which the program data are based are below the poverty line.

MEASUREMENT AND IMPUTATION ISSUES

An analysis by Doyle and Dalrymple (1987) indicates that the manner in which the Census imputes missing data to compensate for income nonreporting probably leads to overestimates of income receipt by some food stamp households.

ERRORS IN PROGRAM DATA

Thus far, the discussion has focused on why the *Census-based* estimates of the proportion of food stamp recipients who live above poverty levels may be too high. Errors in the *program* data also probably account for part of the difference in the findings based on the two data sets. In particular, the income estimates based on program data are almost certainly too low, because income is known to be underreported in Food Stamp Program case records. Food Stamp Program quality control data suggest that approximately 9 percent of households in the program have eligibility or overpayment errors due to income underreporting.[2]

USING POVERTY LEVELS TO SET PROGRAM ELIGIBILITY CRITERIA

The preceding discussion raises a broader issue about the extent to which the official poverty thresholds are a useful starting point for setting eligibility criteria for an assistance program. At one level, the poverty thresholds have a strong intuitive appeal, since they represent a reasonable and widely accepted view of what income levels are low enough to significantly limit a household's ability to meet its basic consumption needs. However, the specific objectives of individual programs often require that operational definitions of income and of eligibility limits differ from those embodied in the poverty levels.

The specific operational requirements of the program have led to using recipient unit definitions and accounting periods that differ from those used in the standard government statistical reports. In addition, as discussed in Chapter II, various Food Stamp Program benefit targeting objectives have led Congress to define food stamp eligibility according to *net* income rather than the *gross* income concept implicit in the poverty thresholds.

The result of these factors is that only a relatively loose connection exists between the poverty standards and Food Stamp Program eligibility limits. Thus, it can be argued that using the poverty standards to specify the program rules is more confusing than helpful.

More generally, this discussion calls into question whether measures of need developed for statistical reporting purposes are useful as the basis for operating public assistance programs. For example, the relatively broad household definition used in the CPS is a reasonable one from the perspective of conducting an overall statistical assessment of the economic levels of U.S. households. However, this definition is not used in the Food Stamp Program because it is not limited to persons who prepare meals together. Similarly, the one-year accounting period in the CPS is a reasonable one for an overall assessment of households' well-being, but it does not provide a sound operational basis for an assistance program designed to respond to short-term needs. Concepts developed for statistical reporting purposes do not always best meet the operational requirements of specific assistance programs.

Notes

1. U.S. Bureau of the Census, "Receipt of Selected Noncash Benefits: 1985," 1987, p. 20.

2. Calculated from Tables 1 and 15 of U.S. Department of Agriculture, Food and Nutrition Service, "Quality Control Annual Report, Food Stamp Program, Fiscal Year 1989," 1990. The estimated percentage of cases with overpayment errors from Table 1 (15.5 percent) was multiplied by the proportion of cases with overpayments for which the case errors involved income data from Table 15 (.587).

SOURCES OF CURRENT INFORMATION ON
THE FOOD STAMP PROGRAM

Changes in federal Food Stamp Program regulations are published in the *Federal Register*, a daily publication of the federal government listing all new federal regulations. This publication is indexed by program. The current regulations are consolidated annually in the *Code of Federal Regulations* (CFR), Title 7, Parts 210–299. Both publications are available at major research libraries or law libraries.

An excellent nontechnical summary of program regulations and statistics, as well as similar information about the other major U.S. low-income assistance programs, is compiled each year in the *Green Book* of the U.S. Congress, House of Representatives, Committee on Ways and Means. This is available in many research libraries and can be obtained from the Government Printing Office in Washington, D.C.

The U.S. Department of Agriculture each year compiles detailed information about the characteristics of food stamp recipient households in "Characteristics of Food Stamp Households." This can be obtained from USDA's Food and Nutrition Service in Alexandria, Virginia.

Monthly program participation statistics can be obtained from the public information service of FNS. These data are also published each month in *Nutrition Week*, published by the Community Nutrition Institute, 2001 S Street NW, Washington, DC 20009.

In addition, *Nutrition Week* frequently includes articles about political and regulatory events relevant to the Food Stamp Program. Information about major political issues related to the program is also occasionally included in articles in the *National Journal* and *Congressional Quarterly*.

Special studies relating to the Food Stamp Program are frequently produced by the following two government organizations: the U.S. Department of Agriculture, Food and Nutrition Office, 3101 Park Center Drive, Alexandria, Virginia 22302; and the U.S. General Accounting Office, Washington, D.C. 20548.

SUPPORTING TABLES

Table C.1 THE FOOD STAMP PROGRAM AVERAGE MONTHLY PARTICIPANTS, 1962–1991

Fiscal Year	Average Monthly Participants
1962	142,817
1963	225,602
1964	336,816
1965	424,652
1966	864,344
1967	1,447,097
1968	2,209,964
1969	2,878,113
1970	4,340,030
1971	9,367,908
1972	11,109,074
1973	12,165,682
1974	12,861,526
1975	16,255,546
1976	17,023,960
1977	15,603,433
1978	14,501,095
1979	15,890,642
1980	19,217,630
1981	20,625,056
1982	19,901,122
1983	21,624,639
1984	20,853,631
1985	19,899,052
1986	19,429,101
1987	19,113,938

(continued)

Table C.1 THE FOOD STAMP PROGRAM AVERAGE MONTHLY PARTICIPANTS,
1962–1991 (continued)

Fiscal Year	Average Monthly Participants
1988	18,644,192
1989	18,764,433
1990	19,930,975
1991	22,568,732
1992	25,367,297

Sources: FY62–FY79 is U.S. Congress, Senate, Committee on Agriculture, Nutrition,
and Forestry, 1985. Pages 167-171.

FY80–FY87 is The Food Stamp Program Information for FY 1980 through FY 1987.
Public Information Data Bank, Data Base Monitoring Branch, Program Information
Division/FM Food and Nutrition Service, USDA, April 1988.

FY88–FY92 is The Food Stamp Program National Data Bank. Program Information
Division, Food and Nutrition Service, January and March 1991, and February 1993.
Puerto Rico numbers are The Food Stamp Program Statistical Summary of Operations,
United States Department of Agriculture, Food and Nutrition Service, 1974–1982.

Note: In 1976 the months of the Fiscal Year changed from August–June to October–
September. Data do not include food stamp participants in Puerto Rico.

Table C.2 FOOD STAMP HOUSEHOLDS WITH SELECTED CHARACTERISTICS 1980–1991

Households with:	1980	1981	1982	1983	1984	1985	1986	1987	1988	1989	1990	1991
Elderly Members	22.6%	20.9%	19.6%	20.2%	22.1%	21.4%	20.2%	20.5%	19.1%	19.5%	17.5%	16.6%
Children	59.9	56.4	58.2	63.8	60.9	59.2	61.2	61.2	60.9	60.1	61.0	61.4
Children Ages 5–17	44.4	41.5	44.2	49.2	47.3	46.3	47.4	47.8	46.6	45.7	46.2	45.5
Earned Income	18.5	19.5	17.6	17.6	19.3	19.6	21.0	20.2	20.0	19.5	19.0	19.8
AFDC or GA	47.2	50.1	50.7	54.8	52.1	49.0	50.3	52.2	51.9	51.3	52.6	50.0

Source: Summer Food Stamp Quality Control Sample, 1980–1991.

Table C.3 PERCENT OF FOOD STAMP HOUSEHOLDS ABOVE THE POVERTY
LEVEL BASED ON NON-ASSISTANCE INCOME, CASH ASSISTANCE,
AND FOOD STAMPS 1991

	Non-assistance Income[a]	Non-assistance + Cash assistance Income[b]	Non-assistance + Cash Assistance + Food Stamps[c]
All Food Stamp Households	3.81%	8.88%	16.27%
Households with Elderly[d]	0.17	16.23	25.88
Households with Disabled, No Elderly[e]	0.07	10.81	22.98
Single Parent with Children[f]	3.35	5.52	11.91
Multiple Adults with Children[g]	9.36	13.74	25.62
Households with Earnings	19.00	24.98	46.10

Source: Summer 1991 Food Stamp Quality Control Sample. Estimates in the table
were calculated by tabulating the numbers of households in various characteristic
groups with various types of income and food stamp receipts which brought them
above the Federal poverty income levels. These counts were then divided by counts
of total households in the characteristic groups.

a. Non-assistance income includes all earned and unearned gross cash income from
private sources, such as household wages, self-employment income, earned income
tax credit, other earned income, household contributions, deemed income, loans, and
other unearned income.

b. Cash assistance income includes all unearned income from government sources,
such as household Aid to Families with Dependent Children, General Assistance,
SSI, Social Security, Unemployment Insurance, Veteran's Benefits, Worker's Compensation, and other government benefits.

c. Food Stamp income is the face value of food stamp benefits.

d. Households with at least one member age 60 or more.

e. Households with SSI income and no member age 60 or more.

f. Households with only one member age 18 or more and children (at least one member
age 17 or less).

g. Households with two or more members age 18 or more and children (at least one
member age 17 or less).

Table C.4 PERCENT OF THE POVERTY GAP FOR FOOD STAMP HOUSEHOLDS
FILLED BY NON-ASSISTANCE INCOME, CASH ASSISTANCE, AND
FOOD STAMPS,[a] 1991

	Non-assistance Income[b]	Non-assistance + Cash assistance Income[c]	Non-assistance + Cash Assistance + Food Stamps[d]
All Food Stamp Households	17.50%	57.95%	77.80%
Households with Elderly[e]	3.66	81.60	91.80
Households with Disabled, No Elderly[f]	4.93	79.01	91.61
Single Parent with Children[g]	14.51	53.05	75.77
Multiple Adults with Children[h]	31.96	61.93	83.71
Households with Earnings	65.55	77.36	96.03

Source: Summer 1991 Food Stamp Quality Control Sample. Estimates in the table were calculated by averaging the relevant types of income and assistance for food stamp households in the various characteristic groups. These averages were then divided by the average poverty levels for households in the groupings.

a. The poverty gap is the amount of income needed to bring poor households up to the poverty line.

b. Non-assistance income includes all earned and unearned gross cash income from private sources, such as household wages, self-employment income, earned income tax credit, other earned income, household contributions, deemed income, loans, and other unearned income.

c. Cash assistance income includes all unearned income from government sources, such as household Aid to Families with Dependent Children, General Assistance, SSI, Social Security, Unemployment Insurance, Veteran's Benefits, Worker's Compensation, and other government benefits.

d. Food stamp income is the face value of food stamp benefits.

e. Households with at least one member age 60 or more.

f. Households with SSI income and no member age 60 or more.

g. Households with only one member age 18 or more and children (at least one member age 17 or less).

h. Households with two or more members age 18 or more and children (at least one member age 17 or less).

REFERENCES

Affholter, Dennis P. and Frederica D. Kramer, eds., *Rethinking Quality Control: A New System for the Food Stamp Program.* Washington, DC: National Academy Press, 1987.

Aiken, John S., et al. "The Impact of Federal Transfer Programs on the Nutrient Intake of Elderly Individuals." *The Journal of Human Resources,* vol. 20, 1985, pp. 383–404.

Allen, Joyce E. and Kenneth E. Gadson. "Nutrient Consumption Patterns of Low-Income Households." Washington, DC: Economic Research Service/USDA, Technical Bulletin no. 1685, 1983.

Allin, Susan, and Harold Beebout. "Determinants of Participation in the Food Stamp Program: A Review of the Literature." Washington, DC: Mathematica Policy Research, Inc., 1989.

Bartlett, Susan, et al. "The Food Stamp Application Process: Office Operations and Client Experiences." Cambridge, MA: Abt Associates, Inc., 1992.

Basiotis, P., et al. "Food Stamps, Food Costs, Nutrient Availability, and Nutrient Intake." *Journal of Policy Modeling,* vol. 9, 1987, pp. 383–404.

Berry, Jeffrey M. *Feeding Hungry People: Rulemaking in the Food Stamp Program.* New Brunswick, NJ: Rutgers University Press, 1984.

Blanchard, L., et al. "Food Stamp SSI/Elderly Cashout." Princeton, NJ: Mathematica Policy Research, Inc., 1982.

Boldin, Paul. "The Distribution of the Shelter Deduction and its Impact on Food Stamp Benefit Amounts." Washington, DC: Mathematica Policy Research, 1987.

Brown, Gregory M. "End of Purchase Requirement Fails to Change Food Stamp Participation." *Monthly Labor Review,* July 1988.

Brown, M., S. R. Johnson, and R. L. Rizek. "Food Stamps and Expenditure Patterns: A Statistical Analysis." University of Missouri-Columbia. Report prepared under U.S. Department of Agriculture Grant No. 53-3244-9-188, 1982.

Burt, Martha R., and Barbara E. Cohen. "Feeding the Homeless: Does the Prepared Meals Provision Help?" Prepared for U.S. Department of Agriculture, Food and Nutrition Service, October 1988.

Burtless, Gary. "The Work Response to a Guaranteed Income: A Survey of Experimental Evidence" in Munnell, Alicia (ed.) *Lessons from the Income Maintenance Experiments*. Boston: Federal Reserve Bank of Boston, 1986.

Butler, J. S., James C. Ohls, and Barbara Posner. "The Effect of the Food Stamp Program on the Nutrient Intake of the Eligible Elderly." *The Journal of Human Resources*, vol. 20, 1985, pp. 405–420.

Chen, J. A. "Simultaneous Equations Models with Qualitative Dependent Variables: A Food Stamp Program Participation and Food Cost Analysis." Ph.D. dissertation. University of Missouri, 1983.

Community Nutrition Institute. "NAS and HHS Caught in New Legal Action Over RDA 10th Edition." *Nutrition Week*, vol. 20, no. 10, March 8, 1990, p. 1.

Corson, Walter, and Walter Nicholson. "An Examination of Declining UI Claims During the 1980s, Draft." Princeton, NJ: Mathematica Policy Research, May 1988.

Davidson, Roger H., and Walter J. Oleszek. *Congress and Its Members, 2nd edition*. Washington, DC: CQ Press, 1985.

Devaney, Barbara, and Thomas Fraker. "The Effect of Food Stamps on Food Expenditures: An Assessment of Findings from the Nationwide Food Consumption Survey." *American Journal of Agricultural Economics*, vol. 71, 1989, pp. 99–104.

————. "Cashing-Out Food Stamps: Impacts on Food Expenditures and Diet Quality." *Journal of Policy Analysis and Management*, vol. 5, 1986, pp. 725–741.

Devaney, Barbara, Pamela Haines, and Robert Moffitt. "Assessing the Dietary Effects of the Food Stamp Program—Volume II: Empirical Results." Princeton, NJ: Mathematica Policy Research, 1989.

Doyle, Pat. "Food Stamp Program Participation Rates, August 1985." Report to Food and Nutrition Service, U.S. Department of Agriculture, Washington, DC: Mathematica Policy Research, 1990.

Doyle, Pat, and Harold Beebout. "Food Stamp Program Participation Rates." Washington, DC: Mathematica Policy Research, November 1988.

Doyle, Pat and Robert Dalrymple. "The Impact of Imputation Procedures on Distributional Characteristics of the Low Income Population." Washington, DC: Proceedings of the Bureau of the Census Annual Research Conference III, 1987.

Esrov, Linda, and SRA Technologies, Inc. "Evaluation of Expedited Service in the Food Stamp Program." Washington, DC: U.S. Department of Agriculture, Food and Nutrition Service, April 1987.

Food Research and Action Center. "Community Childhood Hunger Identification Project: A Survey of Childhood Hunger in the United States." Washington, DC: Food Research and Action Center, March 1991.

Fraker, Thomas M. "The Effects of Food Stamps on Food Consumption: A

Review of the Literature." Washington, DC: Mathematica Policy Research, 1990.

Fraker, Thomas M., and Robert Moffitt. "The Effect of Food Stamps on the Labor Supply of Unmarried Adults Without Dependent Children." Report Submitted to the U.S. Department of Agriculture, Food and Nutrition Service. Washington, DC: Mathematica Policy Research, 1989.

—————. "The Effect of Food Stamps on Labor Supply: A Bivariate Selection Model." Journal of Public Economics, vol. 35, February 1988, pp. 25–26.

Fraker, Thomas M., Sharon Long, and Charles E. Post. "Analyses of the 1985 Continuing Survey of Food Intakes by Individuals—Volume I, Estimating Usual Dietary Intake, Assessing Dietary Adequacy, and Estimating Program Effects: Applications of Three Advanced Methodologies Using FNS's Four-Day Analysis File." Washington, DC: Mathematica Policy Research, 1990.

Fraker, Thomas M., et al. "The Evaluation of the Alabama Food Stamp Cash-out Demonstration, Volume Two: Administrative Outcomes, Overall Conclusions, and Appendices." Washington, D.C.: Mathematica Policy Research, 1992.

Greenstein, Robert. "Universal and Targeted Approaches to Relieving Poverty: An Alternate View." In The Urban Underclass, Christopher Jencks and Paul E. Peterson, eds. Washington, DC: The Brookings Institution, 1991.

Gueron, Judith M. and Edward Pauly. From Welfare to Work. New York: Russell Sage Foundation, 1991.

Hamilton, William L. "Electronic Benefit Transfer in the Food Stamp Program: The Reading Demonstration." Cambridge, MA: Abt Associates, July 1987.

Hamilton, William L., et al. "Factors Affecting Food Stamp Certification Cost." Washington, DC: U.S. Department of Agriculture, Food and Nutrition Service, Office of Analysis and Evaluation, November 1989.

Hollonbeck, Darrell, and James C. Ohls. "Participation among the Elderly in the Food Stamp Program." The Gerontologist, vol. 24, no. 6, 1984, pp. 616–621.

Hollonbeck, Darrell, James C. Ohls, and Barbara Posner. "The Effects of Cashing Out Food Stamps on Food Expenditures." American Journal of Agricultural Economics, August 1985.

Hymans, Saul H., and Harold T. Shapiro. "The Allocation of Household Income to Food Consumption." Journal of Econometrics, Vol. 4, No. 2, 1976, pp. 167–188.

Kondratas, Anna, and Abigail Nichols. "Workfare for Food Stamp Program Recipients, Evidence from Two Sets of Demonstration Projects."

Presentation at the Allied Social Science Association Meetings, December 1987.

Kosterlitz, Julie. "Beefing Up Food Stamps." *National Journal*, February 17, 1990.

Landa, Cady. "Implications of Food Stamp Program Unit Rules: Evidence from SIPP." Washington, DC: Mathematica Policy Research, Inc., 1987.

Leavitt, Thomas D., and James H. Schulz. "The Role of the Asset Test in Program Eligibility and Participation: The Case of SSI." Washington, DC: American Association of Retired Persons, 1988.

Levedahl, J. William. "The Effect of Food Stamps and Income on Household Food Expenditures." U.S. Department of Agriculture, Economic Research Service, Technical Bulletin Number 1794, 1991.

Life Sciences Research Office, Federation of American Societies for Experimental Biology. "Nutrition Monitoring in the United States: An Update Report on Nutrition Monitoring." Prepared for the U.S. Department of Agriculture and the U.S. Department of Health and Human Services. DHHS Publication No. (PHS)89-1255. Washington, DC: U.S. Government Printing Office. September 1989.

Long, Sharon. "Multiple Program Participation Among Food Stamp Participants." Washington, DC: Mathematica Policy Research, Inc., 1988.

MacDonald, Maurice. *Food, Stamps, and Income Maintenance.* New York: Academic Press, 1977.

Maney, Ardith L. *Still Hungry After All These Years: Food Assistance Policy from Kennedy to Reagan.* New York: Greenwood Press, 1989.

Mathematica Policy Research, Inc. "Handbook of Assistance Programs." Prepared for U.S. Department of Agriculture, Food and Nutrition Service, Office of Analysis and Evaluation. Washington, DC: Mathematica Policy Research, 1990.

Maxfield, Myles Jr. "Planning Employment Services for the Disadvantaged." New York: Rockefeller Foundation, 1990.

Melnick, R. Shep. *The Politics of Statutory Rights: Courts and the Congress in the Welfare State.* Washington, DC: The Brookings Institute, forthcoming.

Moffitt, Robert. "Has State Redistribution Policy Grown More Conservative?" *National Tax Journal*, vol. 43, no. 2, June 1990, pp. 123–142.

National Academy of Sciences, National Research Council, Food and Nutrition Board. *Recommended Dietary Allowances, 9th ed.* Washington, DC: National Academy of Sciences, 1980.

National Archives and Records Administration, Office of the Federal Register. *Code of Federal Regulations.* Washington, DC: U.S. Government Printing Office, annual.

Nelson, Lyle, Harold Beebout and Felicity Skidmore. "Economies of Scale in the Food Stamp Program." Washington, DC: U.S. Department of Agriculture, Food and Nutrition Service, Office of Analysis and Evaluation, 1985.

Ohls, James C., et al. "Final Report for the Food Stamp Program Simplified Application Demonstration Evaluation." Washington, DC: Mathematica Policy Research, September 1986.

Ponza, Michael and Linda Wray. "Evaluation of the Food Assistance Needs of the Low-Income Elderly and Their Participation in USDA Programs (Elderly Program Study)." Report to the Food and Nutrition Service, U.S. Department of Agriculture, Washington, DC: Mathematica Policy Research, November 1989.

Puma, Michael J., et al. "Evaluation of the Food Stamp Employment and Training Program." Bethesda, MD: Abt Associates, June 1990.

Ranney, Christine K., and John E. Kushman. "Cash Equivalence, Welfare Stigma, and Food Stamps." *Southern Economic Journal,* vol. 53, no. 4, April 1987, pp. 1011–1027.

Ross, Chris. *Indexing with the Consumer Price Index: Problems and Alternatives.* U.S. Congress, Congressional Budget Office. Washington, DC: U.S. Government Printing Office, 1991.

Ruggles, Patricia. *Drawing the Line: Alternative Poverty Measures and their Implications for Public Policy.* Washington, DC: The Urban Institute Press, 1990.

Ruggles, Patricia and Richard C. Michel. "Participation Rates in the Aid to Families with Dependent Children Program: Trends for 1967 through 1984." Washington, DC: The Urban Institute, 1987.

Rush, David, et al. "Evaluation of the Special Supplemental Food Program for Women, Infants, and Children (WIC)." Report submitted to the Food and Nutrition Service, USDA, under contract 53-3198-9-87. Research Triangle Park, NC: Research Triangle Institute, 1986.

Salathe, Larry E. "The Food Stamp Program and Low-Income Households' Food Purchases." *Agricultural Economics Research,* Vol. 32, No. 4, 1980, pp. 33–41.

Senauer, Ben, and Nathan Young. "The Impact of Food Stamps on Food Expenditures: Rejection of the Traditional Model." *American Journal of Agricultural Economics,* vol. 68, 1986, pp. 37–43.

Smallwood, D. M. and J. R. Blaylock. "Analysis of Food Stamp Program Participation and Food Expenditures." Economic Research Service staff report, U.S. Department of Agriculture, 1983.

Toner, Robin. "New Politics of Welfare Focuses on Its Flaws." *The New York Times,* vol. 141, no. 49,018, July 5, 1992, p. 16.

Trippe, Carole. "Estimating Rates of Participation in the Food Stamp Program: A Review of the Literature." Washington, DC: Mathematica Policy Research, November 1989.

Trippe, Carole, and Pat Doyle. "Food Stamp Program Participation Rates: January 1989." Washington, DC: Mathematica Policy Research, July 1992.

U.S. Bureau of the Census. "Measuring the Effect of Benefits and Taxes on Income and Poverty: 1990." *Current Population Reports.* Series P-60, no. 176-RD. Washington, DC: U.S. Government Printing Office, August 1991.

_____. "Poverty in the United States: 1990." *Current Population Reports,* Series P-60, No. 175. Washington, DC: U.S. Government Printing Office, 1991.

_____. "Receipt of Selected Noncash Benefits: 1985." *Current Population Reports,* Series P-60, No. 155. Washington, DC: U.S. Government Printing Office, 1987.

_____. "Estimates of Poverty Including the Value of Noncash Benefits." Technical Paper Number 55. Washington, DC: U.S. Government Printing Office, 1984.

U.S. Congress, Congressional Budget Office. "The Economic and Budget Outlook: An Update." Washington, DC: July 1990.

_____. "The Economic and Budget Outlook: Fiscal Years 1991–1995." Washington, DC: January 1990.

_____. "The Food Stamp Program: Eligibility and Participation." Washington, DC: November 1988.

U.S. Congress. *Food, Agriculture, Conservation, and Trade Act of 1990.* Public Law 101-624, 101st Congress. November 28, 1990.

_____. *Hunger Prevention Act of 1988.* Public Law 100-435, 100th Congress, 2nd Session. September 19, 1988.

_____. *Food Stamp Act of 1977.* Public Law 95-113, Title XIII. 95th Congress, 1st Session. June 24, 1977.

_____. *Food Stamp Act of 1964.* Public Law 88-525, 88th Congress, 2nd session. June 30, 1964.

U.S. Congress, House of Representatives, Committee on Agriculture. *Food and Agricultural Resources Act of 1990: Report of the Committee on Agriculture to Accompany H.R. 3950 Together with Additional and Dissenting Views.* 101st Congress, 2nd Session. Washington, DC: U.S. Government Printing Office, 1990.

U.S. Congress, House of Representatives, Committee on Ways and Means. *Background Material and Data on Programs Within the Jurisdiction of the Committee on Ways and Means, 1989 Edition.* Washington, DC: U.S. Government Printing Office, 1989.

_____. *1992 Green Book. Washington, DC: U.S. Government Printing Office, 1992.*

_____. *1991 Green Book. Washington, DC: U.S. Government Printing Office, 1991.*

U.S. Congress, Senate, Committee on Agriculture, Nutrition, and Forestry. *The Food Stamp Program: History, Description, Issues, and Options.* Washington, DC: U.S. Government Printing Office, April 1985.

_____. *The Food Stamp Program: History, Description, Issues, and Options.* Washington, DC: U.S. Government Printing Office, April 1985.

U.S. Department of Agriculture, Food and Nutrition Service. "Quality Control Annual Report, Food Stamp Program, Fiscal Year 1989–1990." Program Accountability Division, Quality Control Branch, Statistical Support Section, September 1990–1991.

————. "Food Stamp Program Information for FY 1980 through FY 1990." Washington, DC: Program Information Division, Database Monitoring Branch, July 1991.

————. "Recent Trends in Food Stamp Program Participation: A Preliminary Report to Congress." Prepared by Mathematica Policy Research, Inc. Alexandria, VA: Office of Analysis and Evaluation, July 1990.

————. "Characteristics of Food Stamp Households, 1980–1988." Office of Analysis and Evaluation, 1981–1990.

————. "The Food Stamp Program Quality Control System: A Report to the U.S. Congress." Washington, DC: Office of Analysis and Evaluation, May 1987.

————. "Final Report of the Second Set of Food Stamps Workfare Demonstration Projects." Alexandria, VA: Office of Analysis and Evaluation, 1987.

————. "An Assessment of Nutrition Assistance Programs Including the Procedures Required to Reinstate Direct Commodity Distribution to Needy Households," Washington, DC: Food and Nutrition Service, March 1983.

U.S. Department of Agriculture, Human Nutrition Information Service. Table entitled "Cost of Food at Home Estimated for Food Plans at Four Cost Levels, U.S. Average." HNIS (Adm.) 329, Issued October 1990 and February 1992.

————. "Food Consumption and Dietary Levels of Low-Income Households, November 1979–March 1980," Nationwide Food Consumption Survey, Preliminary Report No. 10. Washington, DC: U.S. Department of Agriculture, July 1982.

U.S. Department of Health and Human Services, Public Health Service. *Healthy People 2000: National Health Promotion and Disease Prevention Objectives.* DHHS Publication No. (PHS) 91-50213. Washington, DC: U.S. Government Printing Office, 1991.

U.S. Department of Health and Human Services, Social Security Administration. *Social Security Bulletin*, vol. 54–55, various issues, 1991–1992.

U.S. Executive Office of the President, Office of Management and Budget. "Budget of the United States, FY 1991." January 1990.

————. "Mid-Session Review of the Budget." July 1990.

U.S. General Accounting Office. "Food Stamps: Reasons for Nonparticipation." Washington, DC: U.S. General Accounting Office, 1988.

————. "Food Stamp Work Requirements: Ineffective Paperwork or Effective Tool?" Report to the Congress by the Comptroller General, April 1978.

The Urban Institute. *The Effects of Legislative Changes in 1981 and 1982 in the Food Stamp Program.* Volume I. Washington, DC: The Urban Institute, 1985.

West, Donald A. "Effects of the Food Stamp Program on Food Expenditures." Agricultural Research Center, Washington State University, Research Bulletin XB0922, 1984.

Zedlewski, Sheila and J. Meyer. *Toward Ending Poverty Among the Elderly and Disabled through SSI Reform.* Urban Institute Report 89-1. Washington, DC: The Urban Institute Press, 1989.

ABOUT THE AUTHORS

James C. Ohls is a senior economist with Mathematica Policy Research (MPR), where he has been conducting research on the Food Stamp Program for 12 years. He is currently completing an evaluation of the effects of a demonstration in San Diego County, California to use checks rather than coupons in issuing food stamp benefits. Other Food Stamp Program issues which he has studied in the past include: program simplification, changes in the benefit determination structure, payment error rates, and administrative costs. His work has involved both extensive statistical analyses of national data sets and also detailed field research at the local office level.

. Dr. Ohls, whose Ph.D. is from the University of Pennsylvania, has also conducted research on a number of other U.S. low income assistance programs, including AFDC, SSI, and the Summer Food Service Program. Prior to joining MPR he taught in the economics department and the Woodrow Wilson School of Public and International Affairs at Princeton University.

Harold Beebout has been studying the Food Stamp Program for nearly twenty years. His simulations of the effects of alternative program changes on recipients and program costs played a critical role in the debates by Congress and the Ford and Carter Administrations leading to the 1977 legislation that established the modern Food Stamp Program. Since then he has directed research on many aspects of the Food Stamp Program including ways to administer the program more effectively and improve program integrity, the effects of converting program benefits from food coupons to cash, and how well the program serves particularly vulnerable populations such as the frail elderly.

Dr. Beebout is currently director of research for Mathematica Policy Research (MPR). Prior to joining MPR in 1974, he directed the transfer income modeling group at the Urban Institute. He received his Ph.D. in agricultural economics from the University of Wisconsin in 1972.

ABOUT THE INSTITUTIONS

MATHEMATICA POLICY RESEARCH (MPR) is an employee-owned social policy research firm established in 1968. It maintains offices in Princeton, New Jersey and Washington, D.C. MPR conducts analysis and evaluation in a broad range of substantive areas, including welfare reform, employment and training, income maintenance, nutrition, child care, education, and health policy. It is known particularly as an innovator in the design and evaluation of evolving public programs.

MPR is committed to providing the policymaking community with the information and knowledge upon which better social programs are built. It provides a broad range of research services, including evaluations of experiments and demonstrations, analysis of the effects of existing policies, survey and other primary data collection, and policy simulation.

THE URBAN INSTITUTE is a nonprofit research and educational organization established in Washington, D.C. in 1968. Its staff investigates the social and economic problems confronting the nation and public and private means to alleviate them. The Urban Institute has three goals for its research and dissemination activities: to sharpen thinking about societal problems and efforts to solve them, to improve government decisions and performance, and to increase citizen awareness of important public choices.

Through work that ranges from broad conceptual studies to administrative and technical assistance, Institute researchers contribute to the stock of knowledge and the analytic tools available to guide decision making in the public interest.

The Institute disseminates its research and the research of others through the publications program of it Press.